Synthetic Painting Media

LAWRENCE N. JENSEN

Chairman, Art Dept., Castleton State College, Castleton, Vermont

Prentice-Hall, Inc., Englewood Cliffs, N.J.

For David and Jane

Current printing (last digit):
13   12   11   10   9   8   7   6

PRENTICE-HALL INTERNATIONAL, INC., LONDON
PRENTICE-HALL OF AUSTRALIA, PTY., LTD., SYDNEY
PRENTICE-HALL OF CANADA, LTD., TORONTO
PRENTICE-HALL OF INDIA (PRIVATE) LTD., NEW DELHI
PRENTICE-HALL OF JAPAN, INC., TOKYO
PRENTICE-HALL DE MEXICO, S.A., MEXICO CITY

Preface

This book is primarily concerned with the recent impact on fine art of the rapidly developing field of the synthetic paint binders and media, together with instructions for their use. The new media have recently exerted a profound influence on the course of modern painting. Today, many painters are employing a great variety of materials where once only pigments were considered feasible. Binders of the six traditional media (fresco, egg tempera, encaustic, oil, watercolor, and pastel) were not capable of adequately holding materials other than pigments to a support. This recent technical development in the fine arts is as important an innovation in our time as the introduction of the oil medium was during the Renaissance.

Each of the major traditional media is discussed in this book with special concern for its advantages and disadvantages relative to the new synthetic media. The conclusions reached indicate that the new media are decidedly superior in many ways.

The answers to the following questions discussed in this book should provide valuable insights for the student, teacher, and painter:

1. How revolutionary is the technical freedom afforded by the new synthetic media?

2. Are painters likely to evolve new forms and modes of expression as a direct result of the widening technical horizon? What light does history throw on this problem?

3. What is the relationship of the artist to his medium? Is it different now than it has been?

4. Does the artist control his medium or does the medium exert its own rationale? Is there an interaction?

5. Can history help us to understand the importance of the artist's medium in relation to his vision of form?

6. Have new media inspired new forms in the past?

7. Have the new synthetic media caused any new directions in contemporary painting?

8. Are there advantages for the art educator in the classroom use of these new media?

9. Will contemporary principles of art education find more fruitful application through the use of these new media? Will creativity be fostered?

10. How are students likely to react to these media?

11. Are there purely technical advantages attending the use of the new media?

12. Are there any disadvantages attending their use?

These and other questions pertaining to the impact of the new synthetic media on contemporary painting are discussed in the following chapters. The technical information provided should enable any serious artist or student to experiment successfully with any of the media described in this book.

Acknowledgments

Because he suggested the idea for this book, I am especially indebted to Ken Riley. Dr. Jack Arends, my patient advisor and friend at Columbia University, was instrumental in guiding both me and the manuscript through the maze of committee hearings and institutional roadblocks that every thesis and doctoral candidate must face. My gratitude also goes to Dr. William Mahoney and Dr. Raymond Patouillet for their steady help and advice.

José Gutiérrez and Alfred Duca deserve special thanks for their willingness in sharing with me and the readers of this book the fruits of their long investigations.

Leonard Bocour and Henry Levison offered liberally of their knowledge and experience in letters and interviews. I am also indebted to Gerould Allyn, Jacques Barzun, John Canaday, Joyce Cary, Maurice Grosser, Ralph Mayer, and Andrew Wyeth, for their permission to borrow some of their ideas.

And finally, Loretta Josselyn must be thanked for her industry in typing the final version of this manuscript in record time.

L.N.J.

Table of Contents

v

1

Introduction

All media, regardless of the age or period in which they are used, exert a profound influence on the artist's attitude toward form. Great traditions and schools of art exemplify ideals in the creation of form that can be traced directly to the medium then in use.

This fundamental concept is especially obvious in the field of architecture. Wood, stone, steel, and reinforced concrete have very different and distinct characteristics as building materials. Great structures created in these materials display, in the builder, a sensitivity and responsiveness to the appropriate use of the materials employed. The materials used in the creation of a significant architectural design strongly dictate the things the artist can and cannot do. Again, the piano has inspired different musical forms than did the earlier harpsichord. In each case, the artist has sought to exploit the potentialities of his chosen medium; the inevitable result is a form appropriate to the technical possibilities and restrictions of the medium used, and of none other. So it is in painting.

This book is primarily concerned with the recent impact on fine art of the rapidly developing field of synthetic media. The history of Western art can demonstrate only two other such profound changes in this technical area. The first is the perfection of the egg tempera technique at the end of the Middle Ages and its ascendency to the position of the most important medium for fine

1

painting. The fresco technique, which is similar to the egg tempera technique, was the dominant medium for mural painting. At the height of the Italian Renaissance, however, travelers from northern Europe began to bring information to the southern masters about a marvelous new medium with an oil base. The introduction of this new medium constitutes the second great technical break-through. The masters of Italy, long dissatisfied with the restrictions imposed by both the egg tempera and fresco techniques, quickly adopted the new oil medium in its many variations. Over the centuries the oil medium has been expanded and developed to meet the esthetic needs of a wide variety of schools and styles of painting.

Not until the twentieth century do we find any significant tendency for artists to begin to explore the potentialities of other media. But as technology made new media possible, serious artists have sought new freedom of expression and have expanded their vision of form. More and more painters have attempted to find their own personal technical means, without traditional reliance on only a few possibilities.

From a technical point of view, all the traditional media have one common characteristic. Each employs pigments in combination with a particular binder. Thus, encaustic paintings combine pigment with wax, fresco paintings combine pigment in aqueous solution with plaster, egg tempera paintings combine pigment with egg yolk, pastel paintings combine dry pigment with a weak solution of gum arabic, watercolor paintings combine pigment with an aqueous solution of gum arabic, and oil paintings combine pigments with oil. As this list readily demonstrates, the ingredient of pigment is constant. The coloring agent may be ground finer or coarser in one technique than in another, but it is pigment nonetheless.

Today, many painters are employing a great variety of materials where once only the use of pigment was considered tenable. Traditional binders were not capable of making materials other than pigments adhere to the support. Now, however, due to the employment of modern synthetic binders, wood, sand, paper, and canvas are some of the most frequently encountered materials used in place of pigment. An increasingly wide variety of other materials are also used. Some have not been employed as successfully as have others, but this may be a measure of the esthetic perceptiveness of the artist, rather than any inherent defect in the materials employed.

The most important result of this new freedom and vitality is a greatly expanded vocabulary for the serious painter. No longer is he limited to a few traditional media with all of the dangers of long established technical clichés and repetitive performances. The sensitive artist today increasingly explores the new media or reworks old media until he has arrived at his own personal technique.

These contemporary explorations have profound implications for the creation of new art forms. This book should amply illustrate the thesis that there is a close relationship between the medium used and the artist's vision. A particular medium can be manipulated to accomplish only a limited number of effects; the artist's vision must find its expression within these limitations.

Historically, each new medium has given rise to a new esthetic. New forms find ready expression within the restrictions and opportunities afforded by the new medium, restrictions and opportunities which are different from those imposed by other media. The six traditional media (encaustic, fresco, pastel, egg tempera, watercolor, and oil) do not exhaust the limits of the possible range of the artist's esthetic vocabulary. Moreover, these media have all imposed severe restrictions of one kind or another.

For the purposes of this book, the concept of the "ideal" medium is often referred to. The ideal medium is hypothetical, but is instinctively felt by most painters. Theoretically, the ideal medium is one that responds to the painter's most subtle thoughts. He need only "think" a passage into being, or have it erased, or darkened, or intensified, or textured, or brightened, or reshaped, and it would be so. No manipulative deficiencies on the artist's part would restrict him. Alterations in color, value, and design could be rapidly experimented with, in a way unlike present procedures that encourage the artist to restrict his vision to present technical commitments. Traditional media fall far short of this ideal, but each successive great medium has tended to move in this direction. Oil is the traditional medium that most nearly approaches these ideal technical requirements, but it also falls far short of their realization. The long history of the development of the oil medium itself, from the Van Eycks to the Abstract Expressionists, has been a movement toward the ideal medium. Technical changes in the formulation of the oil medium as well as changing needs and attitudes account for this gradual improvement.

The artist has always attempted to push back technical barriers that restrict him in the realization of his vision. Today, with the proliferation of new synthetic media, the artist has opportunities to remove some of the restrictions that have shackled him in the past. There are, of course, other considerations than those of a technical nature that have restricted the artist; this book, however, is committed to an analysis of problems and considerations that are essentially technical.

Until the twentieth century, the subject in painting was anecdotal, nature seen poetically, or visions inspired by religion, mythology, and philosophy. During markedly decadent periods the subject was frequently saccharine and sentimental; witness the paintings of Bouguereau and the French Academy during the last half of the nineteenth century. In all instances, whether or not the paintings were good or bad art, the subject was external to the practice or craft of painting itself. The Impressionists, for instance, were not particularly interested in composition or the traditional formal aspects of painting. Their concern was with perception and the immediate transcriptions of a specific visual effect in nature.

Cézanne was the first member of this group to again become passionately involved in the formal considerations of the painter's art; his subjects from nature were merely vehicles for his experiments in design and color. Cézanne was interested in academic theories of composition at first, but he soon discarded these conventions in favor of his own highly original ideas. He limited his space, and conventionalized his drawing. As a direct result of the impact his pictures made on the next generation of painters, Braque and Picasso began to imitate, explore and further stylize Cézanne's conventions of drawing and perspective. The subject of painting became the composition, the design, the study of art itself.[1] The rise of science in the twentieth century, with its implication that appearances are not reality, encouraged artists to discredit the importance formerly given to the visible world. An overriding interest in pure composition soon became the hallmark of modern art. Form became the content, the prime subject, for serious painters.

The medium by which a painter realized his intentions was, until the modern era, a means only. But the turning inward of modern art brought all of the means of picture making into analytical focus. The medium thus became one of the ingredients in a painting which could be considered as an end in itself. Surface became tremendously important.

One of the canons of modern art is the unity of the picture plane, the balanced and equalized emphasis on the painting surface itself. A modern painting is constructed to be an object, not a window on nature. The object is made, in a physical sense, of paint and support.

Painters have always loved the tactile and sensuous qualities of the paint they use, but the modern artist has made the manipulation of pigments, other materials, and medium as seen in the finished work, an end in itself. A typical attitude of the modern artist is expressed by Joyce Cary in his novel *The Horse's Mouth*. Mr. Jimson, the eccentric painter-hero, exclaims, "Paint. Lovely paint. Why, I could rub my nose in it or lick it up for breakfast. I mean, of course, paint that doesn't mean anything except itself."[2]

The modern painter is fascinated by surface and textural effects. He luxuriates in the medium as though it had a mystical identity of its own. Contemporary "Action" painters have perhaps reached the uttermost limits in this direction. For them, the medium and their responses to it, as paint is squirted, splattered, smeared, and sprayed on gigantic canvases, is the totality of the art experience. Design

[1] Maurice Grosser, *The Painter's Eye* (New York: The New American Library, 1956), pp. 129–30.

[2] Joyce Cary, *The Horse's Mouth* (New York: The Universal Library, Grosset & Dunlap, 1957), p. 161.

and the classical formal values count for little or even nothing. The late Franz Kline, an Abstract Expressionist painter, maintained that he was out to destroy any feeling of formal design in his paintings. He wished, in fact, to create "anti-design." Color did not interest him; the problems attending the use of black and white were sufficient. Other painters of this persuasion explore equally occult directions. But the sensuous qualities of paint are central to their enjoyment of the act of painting, as well as to the effectiveness of their finished work.

Not only are many artists turning to synthetic media as binders for a variety of materials other than the traditional pigment, but the support, and even the light by which the artist paints and evaluates his work, are not as they traditionally have been. Panels and canvases have been used for centuries, yet today's painters increasingly use Masonite, a tough, permanent, commercial wallboard. Masonite is not limited to standard stretcher sizes, nor is it as vulnerable to physical damage and accidents or the harmful effects of moisture and humidity as is canvas. Masonite will not split as the traditional wood panel often does.

Picasso is known to prefer artificial light to the traditional north light. He enjoys the heightened sense of excitement not afforded by daylight. Then too, many artists want to paint around the clock, or whenever they are in the mood.

This contemporary phenomenon, an intensified preoccupation with the *means* in the art of painting, is responsible for the artist's interest in the new synthetic media. These binders, because of their unique properties, inspire the artist in new creative directions, with means and ends that were impossible or unthought of in the days when only the traditional media were available. The very great permanence of the new materials is profoundly inspirational; there is the feeling that what one does must be done with all of the ability that the artist is able to muster. The artist's message may endure beyond the life of any previously painted object in art history. There is some of the awesome timelessness of sculpture attending the use of these glass-like, synthetic binders.

The new synthetic media offer significant advantages over traditional media in the field of art education. These advantages are both technical and esthetic. A desirable freedom from technical limitations and restraints attends the use of most of the new media. Traditional instructional media for classroom use, if easy to manipulate, or simply convenient from the point of view of the teacher, are not conducive to rich and varied expression. In the lower grades, the use of crayon, tempera, and watercolor is common. But crayon is severely limited in its range of technical possibilities, while watercolor and tempera, though less limited, are difficult to manage. In the high school, the use of oil paint presents a constant hazard both to the finished work and to the students who may inadvertently brush past. Children, being the unpredictable and volatile individuals they are, make the practice of oil painting an anxious classroom exercise at best.

At the college level, these manipulative problems in the classroom are not as important as they are at the lower levels, but here again, the student is subjected to the traditional limitations imposed by the several standard media. This is not to say that experiences with traditional media and materials must forever be removed from the curriculum. Most serious art students want to understand and be familiar with traditional processes, if not for their own work, then certainly for an appreciation of the vast treasure of the visual arts of mankind. There is every likelihood, however, that the new synthetic media can greatly expand the range of technical possibilities and solutions to esthetic problems, and that the young artist can find a fresher outlet for his creative proclivities through their use, unrestricted by the memory of traditional solutions in traditional media.

The advantages attending the use of the new synthetic media, with special regard to their uses as instructional materials, may be summarized as follows:

1. The new media are inexpensive when compared to traditional classroom art materials.
2. They are fast drying.
3. Their permanency is unmatched by traditional media.

4. The new media may be built up to any thickness without the precautions necessary in traditional techniques.
5. Coloring agents other than pigments can be used with most of the new media.
6. Many of the new media, and all of the most available ones, are nontoxic, given reasonable use, and noninflammable.
7. The new media adhere to a wide variety of surfaces, many of which are far less expensive than the supports required by traditional media.
8. The new media remain unchanged in value and color when dry, if the artist so desires.

Students who have been introduced to synthetic media enthusiastically adopt them. Rather than a contest of technical skill and manipulation, painting classes become exciting laboratories in which creative and experimental work is greatly encouraged by the broad range of effects available in these media. Students who rebel against imitative efforts in traditional media find a vast arena open to them. The ideal medium, one without any technical difficulties or restrictions, is more nearly approached in the new synthetic media. This new freedom is of tremendous assistance to the serious or professional aspirant.

One may well argue that the average interested student without any professional ambitions can profit at least as much as a result of the liberating advantages of the new media. The professional aspirant is willing to practice manipulations and techniques until, after many years, he has gained proficiency and understanding. But the casual enthusiast, the student in required art programs and classes, is impatient with his technical inadequacy. He is easily discouraged. His essential wish is to express himself graphically, to experiment, and to communicate. Media such as watercolor and oil present a seemingly endless series of purely technical problems, impasses which divert the enthusiastic but inexperienced student from a satisfying creative effort.

A case history of one artist's encounter with a synthetic medium can serve to illustrate the profound changes in attitudes, esthetic ideals, and goals made possible by the use of these materials. This is my experience:

In order to make clear the significance to my work of the adoption of the synthetic medium, polymer tempera, the retracing of some of the important turning points in my development as an artist will be helpful. The evaluations are of necessity subjective, but I believe that my experiences are not unusual and will be readily recognized by teachers and students as familiar patterns.

As an adolescent in a New York City high school, I was fortunate in having an art teacher who encouraged his students to paint one full-size watercolor a day. Only in retrospect do I realize that this was a most rigorous and demanding schedule. Since watercolor is such a rapid medium, however, we students accepted this regimen as perfectly normal. We devoted an hour or two every afternoon to this work, and soon acquired a modest skill in the manipulation of the medium.

Each day required the completion of a new design. We soon learned that we could draw upon our experiences and visual memories in a manner unthinkable until that time. We rarely painted from nature, preferring to work up our images from these stored impressions from everyday life. Watercolor is an excellent medium for the beginner despite its technical problems. New starts are constantly demanded. The watercolor painter finds that it is impossible to lackadaisically scrub along day after day on the same tired theme as is often the practice of students working in oil. Relationships are immediately established in watercolor; simple effects quickly bring the work to completion. The watercolor artist is usually disinclined to repaint the same theme again and again in the same way. The artist soon learns that fresh images are far more stimulating, that a night scene holds more interest if the preceding picture was conceived in daylight.

The synthetic media were unknown to us at the time that these watercolor classes were in energetic progress. My contact with these classes lasted from 1940 to 1942. Had the new media been available, they could have been used most effectively in place of watercolor, or perhaps concommitantly. All of the advantages of the watercolor medium as described above are also available in a medium such as polymer tempera. The synthetic media offer this added advantage: the range available to the student is far wider than that which is available in the watercolor medium. The student may work rapidly; he is encouraged to do so as a result of the lack of technical problems. A richness and depth is also available which can stimulate the student beyond the limitations of the watercolor medium. In retrospect, therefore, I believe that my early training at the high school level would have been greatly enriched and expanded if the new synthetic media had been known to us.

During those fruitful high school years we students were encouraged to visit the Metropolitan Museum of Art as well as the group and one-man shows along 57th Street in New York City and elsewhere. Within a short time, most of us had fastened upon a painter hero; in my case the artist was Winslow Homer. Shortly thereafter I discovered the then little-known Andrew Wyeth. Wyeth was more or less a contemporary, only a half dozen years older than I. Watercolor painting soon became for me a medium in which both of these excellent painters seemed to have done everything I could hope to do, and to have done it better. Thereafter, I no longer delighted in my original naive exploits in the watercolor medium. The work of other watercolorists broadened my view of the range of the medium, but for better or for worse, Winslow Homer and Andrew Wyeth remained the masters for me.

After more than a decade of study and the creation of many paintings that were painfully derivative, I was introduced to the synthetic medium, polymer tempera. Since my particular masters worked in other media, I was unable to freely borrow technical mannerisms and clichés as I had so often done in the past. The world had been difficult to see through the eyes of any but Homer and Wyeth; suddenly this crippling influence evaporated. A newly discovered freedom allowed me to develop fresh technical solutions independent of the memories of my two masters, solutions which soon became more than merely technical differences. Attitudes which had been impossible to change while under the spell of my teachers quickly dissolved as I found myself able to design and think through fresh solutions to esthetic problems. My adolescent strengths returned, giving my present work a quality that is uniquely mine.

Although I am not in a position to state unequivocally that my years of apprenticeship could have been reduced, I believe that had I found polymer tempera earlier I might well have found myself as an artist earlier. Art history is replete with painters who never were able to break away from their master's oppressive influence. Could it be that they lacked the freeing influence of a new medium? One can certainly find numerous examples of artists who *did* find a new medium or who used an old one in a fresh, new technique. The identification of the works of many of the world's greatest painters can often best be made by means of their unique paint quality, a characteristic that is frequently obvious at first glance. Van Gogh and Vermeer are extreme examples; most painters follow the same pattern, though more subtly.

Because the synthetic media most nearly approach the ideal medium without technical restrictions of any kind, we may not be too extravagant in supposing that many painters in the near future will find themselves as artists at an earlier age than was the case in the past, when technical manipulations counted for so much. The young painter must certainly be a student for a while; his years of apprenticeship may, however, be reduced, and many more artists may ultimately realize their best potential than has been the case in the past. This is not to say that a change of medium or the use of a new synthetic medium is the only means by which an artist can ultimately reach maturity. The thesis here proposed is that many artists can benefit substantially from the release from old patterns attending the use of any of the new synthetic media, and that new art forms must inevitably result.

2

Traditional Media

N ew art forms arise from new needs and new possibilities. "The two often overlap, and they are brought to the conscious mind by the sudden discovery of new, attractive sensations, of unfamiliar realities, of striking, paradoxical connections in daily experience.[1] Painting media have exerted a profound influence on the character of the forms that have emerged from each succeeding era. Each painting medium, with its individual qualities of brush stroke, color, and texture, produces an effect unique unto itself. In order to more fully appreciate the importance of media and their causal relationship to form in painting, each of the major painting media will be briefly discussed. The media's advantages and disadvantages from a technical point of view will be emphasized, and the most commonly employed manipulations and techniques will be noted. The advantages and disadvantages attending the use of the new synthetic media will be assessed in relation to the traditional media as each is discussed.

Encaustic Painting

Encaustic paintings are made of pigments which are

[1] Jacques Barzun, "Modern Architecture: The Road to Abstraction," *Columbia University Forum,* IV, No. 4 (Fall, 1961), 14.

suspended in hot wax. The technique is very ancient; inscriptions on Doric temple facades testify to its early use. The encaustic technique was usually employed in flat, unmodeled areas, most often as blue or red backgrounds behind figural and ornamental sculptural decorations. Similar remains have been found on Trajan's column in Rome. The Egyptians made frequent use of encaustic techniques in the painting of portraits of the deceased, likenesses which were made to be entombed with the mummified remains. Many excellent examples of Egyptian portraiture are well preserved in many of our museums. Their vigor and freshness are often astonishing.

Historical evidence indicates that encaustic paintings have remarkable lasting qualities. Wax paintings do not turn yellow or oxidize as the oil medium usually does. They retain their body and are impervious to water. Waxes have the highest degree of impermeability to humidity of any of the traditional media. Wax paintings possess a distinctively warm and lustrous surface; the colors appear rich and deep. Some contemporary artists are still attracted to the wax medium. Diego Rivera painted the encaustic mural, "A Flower Festival," for the Ministry of Education in Mexico City. This excellent work is painted in typically bold, flat, strongly patterned, encaustic technique.

The technique of painting with hot wax is as follows: Prepared tablets of pigments mixed with wax are melted and applied to the painting surface (a wall or panel) with heated brushes. The colors must be kept heated on the palette. The heat must be very carefully regulated; too much heat can cause the wax and pigment to separate. After the initial application, the colors are blended with instruments resembling soldering irons, heated over a brazier. Electrically heated spatulas are used by some contemporary artists. The final step is to "burn in" or fuse the surface. The ancients used hot irons held close to, but not touching, the completed painting. Heat lamps are commonly used today for this purpose.

The foregoing should make it clear that although encaustic painting has some distinct advantages over other media, its unwieldiness and inconvenience make it unsuitable to the needs of most contemporary painters. Karl Zerbe, a leading contemporary exponent of the encaustic technique, has discontinued work in hot wax in favor of the new acrylic resin emulsion paints. Many effects easily achieved in other media are either completely beyond the range of encaustic painting or are available only with the greatest of difficulty.

Fresco Painting

Fresco paintings are made by painting on damp plaster with pigments suspended in water. The water evaporates as the lime in the plaster absorbs carbonic acid gas from the air. A glassy skin of crystalline carbonate of lime forms on the surface, making a fresco mural insoluble in water, and at the same time developing the fine sheen peculiar to genuine fresco painting.

Like encaustic painting, fresco painting is an ancient technique. The earliest known fresco paintings of great quality are those of the late Minoan period, excavated at Knossos in Crete. After more than three thousand years, the available fragments are still hard and resistant to severe exterior conditions. No Hellenic Greek fresco paintings exist today, although they are reported to have been painted. Rome made great use of the fresco technique, as did the muralists of the Italian Renaissance.

Fresco painting has always been a mural technique. Not until modern times and the discovery of the new synthetic media has the pure fresco method of mural painting been seriously challenged. José Gutiérrez has been instrumental in developing a group of media which have almost completely replaced the fresco technique in Mexico. Many other painters around the world are now adopting his methods.

Fresco painting has demonstrated its great durability. Moreover, the fresco technique is ideally suited to the esthetic requirements of mural painting, a painting style which must be thoroughly in harmony with the surrounding architecture. Modeling is usually kept to a minimum. Flat color areas and a strong linear pattern are typical. The fresco mural is part of the interior or exterior wall surface of a building and must be controlled by its location, by considerations of scale, and by its readability from many different angles and distances. Clarity and simplicity are essential.

Great examples of mural painting in the fresco technique abound. The murals of Pompeii, Giotto's great achievements, the masterpieces of Piero and Mantegna, as well as Michelangelo's Sistine Chapel, all testify to the greatness of the fresco medium.

The technique of painting in the fresco medium is exceptionally demanding, requiring great care in the selection of the materials to be used. The wall on which the mural is to be painted must receive special and painstaking preparation, and the design must be thoroughly worked out in full scale before the work can proceed. Next, the design must be transferred to the plaster wall, section by section as the work progresses, beginning at the upper left corner in order to prevent dripping on finished work. Each day's work must be preceded by a final coat of plaster which must not be too wet when the actual application of the colors begins. Watercolors are applied to the fresco wall with the tip of the brush in a single-stroke, hatching technique. Seams between each day's work must be planned to fall at the least conspicuous places, usually along contour lines of the composition. Unused plaster must be cut away before the following day's work can proceed. No retouches are possible for about four weeks, when casein paints may be used sparingly.

Much detailed instructional material is available for those who would attempt a mural in the fresco technique. All of it emphasizes the care that is necessary; for casual experimentation, such as is commonly practiced in the oil medium, fresco painting is not recommended. The high order of planning involved in the making of a fresco is one of this technique's disadvantages from the point of view of contemporary esthetic standards. Most contemporary works are improvised to a greater or lesser extent. Picasso's "Guernica" could not have been revised and reworked if it had been made as a fresco.

The impurities in the air of today's cities, acid-bearing fumes and smoke, have a distinct tendency to deteriorate the fresco surface. Many indoor fresco paintings have been preserved very well; outdoor fresco paintings are unable to withstand the rigors of wind, sun, rain, and snow. True fresco paintings are not portable except with the greatest of difficulty. As a result, the fresco mural usually suffers the fate of the building for which it was created, a profound disadvantage in the minds of many artists and art lovers. Leonardo's "Last Supper" is a typical victim of this eventuality.

The very restrictive technical requirements of fresco painting, only summarized here, enforce attitudes about form within very specific boundaries. Contemporary painters have turned to media with less rigorous technical restrictions; the modern synthetic media lead the list of painting materials now employed in the painting of murals.

Egg Tempera Painting

Egg tempera paintings are made by painting on panels with pigments suspended in a mixture of water and egg yolk. Although there are hundreds of formulas available for the concoction of egg and oil emulsions, egg yolk and egg white combinations, as well as varnish and gum recipes, the majority of writers on technical matters are of the opinion that the pure egg yolk and water medium provides the best tempera emulsion. The special character of egg tempera rests on the fact that it is an emulsion. An emulsion is a mixture which combines fatty, oily, resinous, or waxy ingredients with a watery liquid. There are a great many emulsions existing in a natural state; milk and egg yolk are familiar examples. These natural emulsions become insoluble in water upon drying. Egg tempera films are also tough, leathery, and very permanent.

The egg tempera medium is generally associated with the Italian Renaissance, a time when it was the foremost medium for easel painting. Some use in medieval times, however, preceded this golden age of tempera painting. Cimabue (1240–1301) and Duccio (1255–1319) are early masters of the egg tempera medium; Botticelli (1444–1510) and Mantegna (1431–1506) are typical of the later Renaissance egg tempera masters. Tempera paintings by

(Andrew Wyeth: *Ground Hog Day*, 1959; Philadelphia Museum of Art)
Fig. 1 "Ground Hog Day," by Andrew Wyeth. A masterful example of contemporary egg tempera painting.

these great masters are noted for their brilliant, luminous crispness, a quality impossible to imitate in any other traditional medium. The dried paint film does not darken or yellow with age as faulty oil paintings habitually do; on the contrary, the egg tempera paint film becomes brighter as the gesso ground on which tempera paintings are usually executed gradually becomes more evident. Incorrectly painted egg tempera paintings have the advantage of showing their defects upon thoroughly drying; corrections can then be made. "When a true tempera is done it should be entirely opaque. Only in this way can you obtain that beautifully fabricated surface one associates with the best egg tempera paintings."[2] Like fresco and encaustic painting, the egg tempera medium is not suited to the casual experiments of the weekend painter, nor is it a useful medium for instruction in the average classroom.

Compared to fresco painting, egg tempera painting is a relatively simple matter. The formidable reputation of the traditional egg tempera technique is due to the thorough planning necessary, and to the meticulous brush manipulations of the masters. Andrew Wyeth, the foremost contemporary painter in the egg tempera medium, has instructed me as follows:

Selected colors should be ground and mixed into a paste-like substance in distilled water, and stored in air-tight jars until needed. These colors will keep indefinitely. Permalba, an excellent white pigment used in tempera painting, is easily mixed as it is needed.

The painting should be executed on a gesso ground. The composition is laid in with charcoal and then carefully drawn over with India ink. It is important to develop as much form as possible at this stage. Richness in the dark tones is dependent upon the ink underdrawing. When the ink drawing has been worked up to full tonal strength, the artist should next brush the entire panel with a coating of egg yolk and water. The usual mixture is one-third distilled water and two-thirds egg yolk. The yellowing effect of the yolk of hens' eggs disappears rapidly and offers no problems.

A common practice is to first lay in the colors transparently, as one would paint a watercolor. Opacity is built up as the painting progresses. Glazing with the egg medium and transparent color can help to develop richness. An egg tempera painting typically exhibits a strong linear pattern because of the difficulty encountered in the blending of the colors. If sufficient attention is given to its execution, however, an egg tempera painting can exceed in quality anything one can do in oils. This high level of quality is the charm of so many exquisite egg tempera panels from the great days of the Italian Renaissance to the present.[3]

[2] Andrew Wyeth, letter to the author, October 28, 1943.
[3] Andrew Wyeth, letter to the author, November 30, 1943.

The egg tempera medium has some disadvantages other than the meticulous technique required. This medium, like the encaustic and fresco mediums, is limited in its range of effects, especially when compared to the oil medium. If egg tempera is glazed or over-painted with oil paint, as was the practice of many of the painters who worked at the height of the Renaissance and later (Leonardo and El Greco are typical), the egg medium is subject to all of the ills of the oil medium. However, a tempera underpainting is perhaps more suitable than oil for receiving thin layers of oil color in glazes and scumbles.

Historically, the decisive disadvantage of the egg tempera medium has been the inflexibility of the egg film, together with the great amount of time required to cover a given area. As artists competed for larger and larger commissions, painters employing the oil medium quickly out-produced the egg tempera practitioners. Tremendous oil paintings could be rolled and transported, satisfying the new demand for the flamboyant and the spectacular. The Van Eycks and others in the north continued to paint with the oil medium in the meticulous manner of the egg tempera technique, but even in this imitative style, the oil medium was far more flexible and more rapid of execution. The classic era of the egg tempera medium was at an end.

Today, the new synthetic media can reproduce effects long thought to be attainable only in the egg tempera medium. The great advantage of the new media lies in their ability to circumvent most of the technical difficulties of the older medium. Should the artist so desire, paintings with all of the qualities of traditional egg tempera can be created in very much less time, and on a scale hitherto believed impossible.

Pastel Painting

Pastel paintings are made by drawing with pigments bound tenuously together by a gum solution or other weak binder. The process dates back more than 200 years, if we are to exclude prehistoric drawings made on cave walls with chalks and earths. Draftsmen of the Italian Renaissance, such as Michelangelo, frequently made chalk drawings, but the appearance of a painted surface in full color did not emerge until the eighteenth century. At that time, men of the stature of Chardin, Watteau, and Boucher were working in the medium. The Impressionists made great and varying use of colored chalks; Redon, Renoir, Degas, Toulouse-Lautrec, and Manet are among the most famous masters of the pastel medium.

Pastel is a remarkably permanent medium. The lack of a binder holding the colors together or to the support make this medium unique. Mechanical injuries are the medium's chief enemy; it will neither yellow nor crack nor exhibit the multitudinous defects associated with the traditional binders. The colors are intense, surpassing any other medium in this regard. Degas and others have used the pastel medium in association with the oil and tempera media. Some contemporary artists are experimenting with pastel in combination with a synthetic tempera medium, Rhoplex AC-33. Although pastel is capable of very fine detail, most practitioners use the medium in such a way as to take advantage of pastel's color brilliance and loose, spontaneous effects.

Both Doerner and Mayer are somewhat suspicious in regard to commercially available pastel chalks. Some colors are compounded of fugitive dyes and therefore quickly fade. Both authors recommend that the serious artist make his own pastel sticks, noting that the great variety of colors on the market are unnecessary since any variation from the most intense hue of each color can easily be made on the spot. Detailed directions are available in the books by both Doerner and Mayer.

Once one has decided on the color sticks to be used, the actual technical process is very simple, simpler in fact than any other important medium. The pigments will cling to almost any soft paper or textured surface. The colors are applied directly and boldly. A variety of manipulations are possible with stumps, bristle brushes, and the hand and fingers working directly into the pigment. Pastels are often done on a sloping easel leaning toward the artist at the top in order that the dust from the tenuously bound pigments will fall away from the picture surface. Pastels are usually sprayed with fixative. Many artists, however, prefer to glass pastel paintings, leaving them unfixed in order to preserve subtleties obscured to some extent by the fixing process.

Pastel colors reflect only surface light. This effect is almost identical with the appearance of dry pigment, and is responsible for the special quality of pastel painting. This unique characteristic can also be considered a disadvantage. No glazing is possible in the pure pastel medium; color depth due to complex reflections from lower layers of pigment are therefore beyond the resources of the medium. Since many painters consider scumbling and glazing to be the richest technical resources available to the artist, the inability of the pastel medium to achieve these effects has prevented it from becoming as popular as is the oil medium.

The new synthetic media cannot compete with the special qualities available through the use of a binder-free medium. However, as suggested by the work of Bittleman, synthetic binders may be found very helpful in preserving the finished work from mechanical damage. New forms are likely to find easy expression in the pastel medium as the highly transparent synthetic media encourages new methods of application. There is reason to believe that glazing and scumbling will become available to the painter in pastels as these new directions are explored.

Watercolor Painting

Watercolor paintings are made by painting on a white surface with finely ground pigments suspended in an aqueous solution of gum arabic. From the earliest times painters have had watercolor kits that were compact and easy to carry about. Although ivory and other materials were once used as the support for watercolor painting, rag papers specially prepared for the medium are preferred today. The watercolor technique is based on the glazing ability of thinly applied color, and is typically used by contemporary artists in a rapid, spontaneous technique. Although outdoor sketching has long been the major use of the medium, early watercolor painting in Europe imitated the finish and tightness of the oil and tempera media. Before the discovery of photography, a school of miniature portrait painting on ivory flourished. Rembrandt is famous for his very freely brushed watercolors of figures and glimpses of nature. They were not painted in full color, however, but were brushed in with a single pigment.

The American watercolorists were the first artists to explore extensively the use of the medium in a full range of color, employing a spontaneous and painterly technique. Winslow Homer is considered by many to be the father of American watercolor painting; his Bahamian and Adirondack watercolors have never been surpassed for their simplicity, brilliance, directness of observation, and technical mastery. Chinese, Korean, and Japanese painters have utilized a watercolor technique for centuries, but they do not paint in the fully developed, free style of the West. Their work is inclined to stylization, but is excellent within its limits.

The ground in watercolor painting determines to a very large extent the ultimate effect as well as the longevity of the work. Handmade papers of linen rags are considered to be the best supports. If the colors selected are not fugitive, and the ground is made of quality materials, watercolor paintings can maintain their original freshness indefinitely. Watercolors are always glassed because of their great vulnerability to moisture and air pollution. Dust, grease, and acids can quickly yellow and stain an unprotected watercolor.

The watercolor technique is actually very simple, but because of the inability of the medium to accept changes and corrections gracefully, the most approved method is spontaneous and direct. Tricks are frowned upon, although a great variety of clever manipulations are possible. The watercolor medium has been employed most successfully by artists who use the paints in a highly developed sketching technique. Watercolors are not well adapted to thoughtful studies requiring considerable time and a flexible, easily corrected technique. One of the most common objections to the medium is the difficulty encountered by most artists in the development of the necessary control. Because of this problem, as well as the sketchy nature of the finished product, watercolor painting has never been classed with the major mediums, as oil, fresco, and egg tempera commonly are. Great works in the watercolor medium are rare.

The acrylic resins have been used by some painters in techniques closely resembling those of watercolor painting. There is every reason to believe that some of the difficulties attending the use of the watercolor medium can be eliminated. The most hopeful direction is the development of methods that will allow corrections without hindering the ultimate effect. Longevity of the paint film may also be enhanced by the use of synthetic binders rather than the traditional gum arabic.

Oil Painting

Oil paintings are made by painting with pigments suspended in oil or an oil base medium, such as a mixture of oil, varnish, and turpentine. A great variety of materials has been used for the oil painting support, but canvas and wood panels are preferred. Hubert Van Eyck (1370–1426), a Flemish master, is popularly accredited with the discovery of oil painting. Doerner points out, however, that the "discovery" of oil as a superior binder was more likely the result of logical and effective employment of the materials then in use. Many artists, including Leonardo da Vinci, experimented with the addition of oils to tempera in an effort to expand the technical range and the expressive potentialities of the traditional egg tempera medium. One of Leonardo's most famous experiments, his "Last Supper," developed major irreparable defects during his lifetime.

Ever since oil painting's initial popularity, the medium has remained the foremost technique for fine painting. Mayer points out that, "Although all the other techniques are practiced for certain advantages they have over oil painting, the latter remains standard because the majority of painters consider that its advan-

tages outweigh its defects and that in scope and flexibility it surpasses watercolor, tempera, fresco and pastel."[4] Because oil is
the standard contemporary medium, the purposes of this book
will be best served by considering the qualities that make this
medium unique. Although it is possible and even likely that the
new synthetic media will develop standards superior to those now
held by the oil medium, all new media must first be compared
to the standards long associated with oil painting. Only by meet-
ing these traditional standards will the new synthetic media gain
wide acceptance and appreciation for the excellent qualities they
possess.

The primary advantages of the oil painting medium over other
permanent and traditional painting techniques are:

1. The oil painting medium offers the greatest flexibility of any
   of the media discussed. It is easily manipulated and is
   adaptable to a wide range of effects.
2. The oil technique is capable of combining body color, glazes,
   and opaque or transparent effects in full range in the same
   painting.
3. Oil colors change very little on drying. This cannot be said
   of most other media. The artist is very greatly aided by
   a technique that allows him to place one color or tone
   against another with the certain knowledge that neither will
   change when dry.
4. Because of the flexibility of the oil paint film, large paintings may be executed on canvas, rolled, and easily transported.
5. The oil medium is slow drying. This allows time to blend
   color for smooth effects, and also permits additions and
   corrections.
6. The oil painting medium is universally accepted by the artists
   and the public. This acceptance has resulted in public confidence in the essential quality of oil painting, and at the

[4] Ralph Mayer, *The Artist's Handbook,* rev. ed. (New York: The Viking
Press, 1957), p. 129.

same time has created a world-wide supply of standardized oil paints, a great aid to the artist.[5]

These striking advantages of the oil medium are not gained without some very serious disadvantages. The oil medium darkens and yellows with age. Paint films made of oily ingredients are very vulnerable to injuries to the tonal and color structure of a painting. Cracking and flaking may also occur. The main result of these technical defects is that very few oil paintings have come down to us through the centuries without major attempts at restoration, usually by men far below the competence level of the masters who originally created these great works. This major limitation of the oil medium is one of the foremost reasons why many contemporary painters are searching for a new binder, a medium that will combine some of the advantages of oil and yet not be susceptible to the disastrous defects mentioned above.

The artist must realize that these technical considerations do not affect the level of excellence of the art product at the time that it is created, but that the longevity of the work may be strongly affected by the technical procedure employed. Albert Pinkham Ryder's wonderful pictures have rapidly deteriorated over a relatively short period of time because of his violation of proper technical procedures. Had he been able to paint with one of the new synthetic media, there is every reason to believe that his particular esthetic goals could have been achieved without violation of safe technical procedure. Many painters of the late nineteenth century uncritically made use of the newly available commercial oil paints, paints that were often very inferior to the traditional hand-ground colors. The deterioration of some of the works of such painters as Winslow Homer and Vincent van Gogh has been attributed to this cause.

Commercially available oil paints have continued to be a source of trouble to the conscientious painter. Various adulterants and extenders have been added to the tube colors since they first appeared on the market. This practice is often necessary in order

[5] Mayer, *The Artist's Handbook,* p. 130.

to prevent the pigment and oil from separating in the tube and also to enable the manufacturer to use less expensive fillers in place of the more expensive pigments. These changes from the traditional hand-ground method of manufacturing oil colors are not designed to be of particular advantage to the painter, but are the result of the manufacturer's wish to make a less expensive product that will keep indefinitely on the merchant's shelf. Paint

(The Metropolitan Museum of Art, Samuel D. Lee Fund, 1934).

Fig. 2 "Moonlight Marine," by Albert Pinkham Ryder. An oil painting by the famous American painter.

made by these commercial methods does not dry to as tough a film as did the traditionally formulated paint. Oil paint is intrinsically much more transparent than one who has not worked in the oil medium would suppose. The new adulterants have made it still thinner. Because the paint film contains less pigment in proportion to its bulk, it is much less opaque, and must be applied more thickly. In order to paint over these thick layers of wet paint without picking them up, one must use a heavily loaded bristle brush. The brushes must be large; wet oil paint applied with small brushes on top of thick, wet oil paint results in muddy tones and an unpleasant, troubled surface. The brushes must be of bristle because the softer camel's hair or sable will not hold enough paint for the necessary loaded brush stroke.[6]

The technique of oil painting cannot be approached casually if permanent results are desired. Deterioration of the oil paint film will be hastened if the artist does not carefully construct his work. A white ground is considered to be the best; the material is usually gesso. This is because the aging paint film becomes more and more transparent; the light ground keeps the picture fresher looking and tends to counteract the darkening of the oil medium.

A maxim learned by all painters who employ the oil medium is that one must not paint "lean over fat" or "short over long." This implies that the upper layers of paint must be as flexible and susceptible to the same degree of expansion and contraction as the undercoats. The underpainting must be lean; subsequent layers of paint must be richer in oil content.

An added complication results from what is known as the "oil index," described in detail in Mayer's book. Pigments vary in their ability to absorb linseed oil as they are ground into a usable, pasty consistency. Mayer's index lists the well-known pigments and ascribes a value to each according to its ability to absorb oil. This is very important knowledge with which the painter must be familiar as he works, because it is not good practice to employ

[6] Grosser, *The Painter's Eye*, p. 66.

pigments of high oil absorbency as underpainting for colors having a low absorbency rating. Few painters today are aware, for instance, that it is technically unsound to paint emerald green over burnt umber, or yellow ochre over viridian. The dangerous combinations, as listed by Mayer, number over 200![7] The complications are such that it is frequently a matter of luck as to whether an oil painting will long survive or not.

Although the oil medium is subject to cracking, flaking, yellowing, and darkening, if a painting is carefully constructed according to sound principles, these defects can be minimized. The long history of oil painting indicates, however, that few painters were able to maintain this high level of craft. There are Rembrandts that are in remarkable condition and others that are far from satisfactory. Restorers, of course, are frequently to blame, but their employment is encouraged by the owner's wish to "freshen up" deteriorated oil paint films. Egg tempera paintings, because they tend to grow lighter with the years, have not been so constantly and disastrously tampered with. The chapters devoted to the new synthetic media will attempt to demonstrate that most, if not all, of the disadvantages inherent in the oil medium can now be eliminated. Moreover, the new media have advantages beyond the range of the traditional oil medium; these, too, will be discussed.

Traditional Practices

The six traditional media discussed here have been the dominant materials employed by artists in the creation of works of art painted on a two-dimensional surface. These six media have not been challenged as materials for artistic painting until very recently. "From the point of view of permanence, all of these accepted and time-tested media can be considered of equal merit."[8] This means, of course, that all six media have some undesirable characteristics in relation to permanence, defects which the care-

[7] Mayer, *The Artist's Handbook*, p. 145.
[8] Mayer, *The Artist's Handbook*, p. 129.

ful painter does his best to minimize. Materials for each medium must be carefully selected; oil paint, egg tempera, encaustic, and fresco must be carefully manipulated and applied if they are to remain in reasonably good condition. The fragility of watercolors and pastels, media which do not have the particular disadvantages of the preceding four, require that they be very carefully preserved.

As this discussion has sought to demonstrate, each medium has its own characteristic appearance and manipulative advantages and disadvantages. There is a distinct tendency for artists to value and seek after as unrestrained a technique as possible within the restrictions imposed by each of the six media. All media can be handled with great care and meticulousness, but an experienced master tends to become impatient with a too niggling technique; some media lend themselves to very precise control with less effort than do others. In general, however, each medium tends to be used as freely and as directly as is technically possible. Not only does this technical development toward a freer style occur within the careers of individual artists (Titian and Degas are typical examples), but entire schools of painting frequently show a trend from a cautious use of a particular medium toward greater freedom and spontaneous expressiveness. Schools of painting as divergent as those of the Italian Renaissance and the current New York school of Abstract Expressionists demonstrate this tendency. The history of the development of the oil medium from the careful work of the Van Eyck brothers to the dynamic brush work of the Venetian school is another case in point.

As a result of this drive toward the most unrestrained use of a particular medium, all media tend to be known by their characteristics when freely employed. For example: egg tempera is not conducive to the painting of large, simple areas (as is fresco) or to translucence and re-working (as is oil on canvas). If egg tempera is handled too freely, it loses its essential beauty and esthetic advantages; if the rendering becomes too spontaneous, other media can do the job better. As a result of this drive toward the optimum level of free manipulation in the egg tempera medium, a characteristic repertoire of brush strokes has been developed. The opaqueness of the medium is retained while the brush strokes do not vary greatly from painting to painting. They would never be confused with the brush strokes typically found in paintings of any of the other five great media.

Attitudes toward form have been fashioned in no small degree by the limits of the medium employed. If an effect can be achieved beautifully and easily in a particular medium, it is very likely that it will become a standard practice. In the interest of consistency, a hallmark of any art, only those things will be done which harmonize with manipulations previously found to be simple, beautiful, and easy of execution. Textural effects are introduced within this framework which quickly become familiar as typical of the particular medium. Color, too, is controlled by the requirements of available pigments (lapis lazuli placed its special stamp on many early masterpieces), and by the tendency to exploit whatever can create the best effect. Thus an attitude toward form becomes part of the expressiveness of a medium.

This attitude toward form, once it has gained its position in the mind of the artist, not only leaves its imprint on forms as they are conceived and painted, but also influences the artist in his *selection* of forms from nature. This phenomenon can be best illustrated in a difficult medium like watercolor, in which each artist works out a shorthand for the rendering of particular forms. These medium-dependent forms are repeated in painting after painting. Similar examples abound throughout the long history of painting, architecture, and sculpture. The wider range of most other media has allowed the artist to develop a wider range of interpretations; the influence of many media is thus more subtle than that of the highly restrictive watercolor.

There are those who insist that the very difficulties and limitations of a medium can help to impose a unity that can elevate a work of art. A teacher will often notice that relatively inferior student sketches can be transformed by the technical limitations of the silk-screen process. A lecturer in fine arts at Columbia University once made the point that the ceiling of the Sistine Chapel was such an unlikely place to paint a fresco, that the very severe restrictions imposed by this awkward combination of support and medium helped Michelangelo transcend his own great gifts. In short, the medium tends to shape the artist's vision of what he can and cannot do.

Many artists will argue, however, that a medium of great potential range is of tremendous assistance in freeing the painter from clichés and stylized nuances. Historically, the oil painting medium has been such a freeing agent. A wide variety of attitudes and needs have found their expression through the oil medium.

The history of Western painting clearly demonstrates the changing attitudes and ideas held by succeeding schools of artists in relation to form. The works of art reveal that the most significant changes have occurred at the same time as the introduction of a new medium, or a new way of working with an old medium. This thesis is most clearly demonstrated by noting the profound changes that occurred with the introduction of the oil medium at the height of the Italian Renaissance. Schools of art ultimately induce reactions to the prevailing, popular theories and attitudes; rebellious artists experiment with new techniques as part of their search for a new idiom. The careful working-out of the laws of perspective caused an impact on succeeding schools of art similar to the changes wrought by the introduction of a new medium. A new painting medium is as significant to the artist's vision of form in painting as is a new building material to an architect's solution of formal problems in architecture.

At the same time that Masaccio in Italy was completing his great works in the fresco medium, the Van Eyck brothers in northern Europe were experimenting with their improved oil formula. Variations on these early and successful formulas were used by Leonardo and Raphael almost a century later, at the height of the Italian Renaissance. Linear rigidity was the constant characteristic of form in painting preceding the discovery of the oil medium. Attempts had been made to enlarge the range of egg tempera, but the technical problems presented by the medium enforced a strongly linear character. Here, as is always the case, the materials the painter used dictated main elements of his painting style; fresco as well as egg tempera are rigid by nature.

The softening of edges was the first important change encouraged by the new medium of oil. Although, because of long habit and tradition, the new oil paintings were still planned in the manner enforced by the egg tempera medium, a new softness became immediately apparent. The "Mona Lisa" by Leonardo, painted about 1502, is considerably less rigid than Jan Van Eyck's "The Betrothal of the Arnolfini," painted in the year 1434. Both, however, owe a great deal to the careful planning and underpainting so typical of the egg tempera tradition. The oil medium in that period, although profoundly altering the artist's ability to render form, was still far from a fully developed medium.

The Venetian masters wrought another great change, advancing beyond men like Leonardo and Raphael, who employed the oil medium as if it were only a richer way of painting in tempera. The great masters of the Venetian school, men such as Titian and Tiepolo, soon lost every tempera characteristic. The oil medium became a large, free, loose, and easy way to work. Forms became more varied along their edges, while the brush stroke itself became the very signature of a master. This is still the prevailing style today, more than four hundred years later.

The fullest potentialities of the oil medium, however, were not to be realized until the middle of the nineteenth century. From Cimabue to Ingres, the finished painting in any medium owed its structure to a carefully planned underpainting, preceded by numerous studies. According to Cennino Cennini, Cimabue made his underpainting in brown, white, and green, in the egg tempera medium. Ingres underpainted in black and white, although he worked in the oil medium. The planned picture had remained basic to all serious painting up to that time, no matter what medium was used; all the great masters approached the problem of a fully colored rendering in the same way. The problems of drawing, designing, and tonal relationships were solved in the cartoon and study stage. What had been decided upon was then incorporated into the underpainting in a value rendering. An ink underdrawing was frequently the first step in the building up of an underpainting in egg tempera. The oil painters found that ink was unnecessary because of the relative opacity of the oil medium, and underpainted in what came to be known as the "dead painting," because of its gray and lifeless appearance. Before the picture in oil could be continued, it was imperative that the underpainting be completely dry. When the oil medium was first introduced, the painters timidly glazed and thinly painted over the underpainting, but with the Venetian experience, paint was soon loaded onto the canvas. Some of the underpainting was permitted to show through, especially in the shadow areas. A feeling of depth was created in this manner that no other method could provide. The problems attending the use of full color were thus separated from the problems of drawing, modeling, and designing.

The planned picture offered the advantages of an orderly procedure as well as the separation of the major problems encountered in the creation of a painting. This traditional method remained in vogue for almost three hundred years, until well after the discovery of photography and the rise of the Impressionists. Paintings from these earlier centuries all exhibit a respect for the world of visual reality. Perhaps this is due in part to the separation of the problem of drawing from the process of finishing the painting in full color. Even today, realists like the painter Andrew Wyeth, and the illustrator Ken Riley, still make use of the planned method, believing that it affords them greater control.

Until the Impressionists, the oil medium was used for serious painting only in the studio. Watercolor and oil were sometimes used for sketching outdoors, but the results were never considered anything more than studies useful for future reference.

After the development of commercially prepared tube paints in the early 1840's (Winsor and Newton adopted the collapsible tin tube in 1841), painters found the adulterants added by the manufacturer made painting over an oil underpainting very inconvenient. The commercial manufacturer needed a very slow drying paint in order to prevent hardening in the tube. These slow drying colors were quite satisfactory for *alla prima* painting, but the carefully built-up planned picture became all but impossible with these new materials.[9]

A profound technical breakthrough resulted from the development of tubed oil colors. The new paints were both portable and slow drying; artists began to paint outdoors without a preconceived plan. Many new ideas about form quickly asserted themselves, and both Corot and Courbet became the first masters of the new vision. Both painters worked from the human model and nature, outdoors in the bright light. The first sharp impression of the image from nature was not obscured by the old method of working from drawings.

The transition from the studio to painting on location outdoors was admittedly a profound one, but the very character of the newly available commercial paints was even more striking. The older hand-made paints were applied thinly because they covered so well; their pigment content was relatively high. The new paints were heavily adulterated, enforcing a heavily loaded brush stroke in order to compensate for less pigment. Because of the slow drying nature of the new paint, it was inadvisable to make corrections over freshly applied passages. The scraping off of unsatisfactory areas was preferred. Such a technique put a premium on rapidly executed, freely and heavily brushed pictures. Problems of the rendering of form were solved within this technical restriction.[10]

The Impressionist movement began as a revolt against the planned picture, but within a very short time the whole body of academic tradition was discarded. Impressionist paintings were reviled by the official critics essentially because they were unpremeditated, audacious sketches, lacking an elevating and classically acceptable theme. The special character of the new tube paints had made all this possible. The term applied to this revolutionary style was still "oil painting," but there remained little in common with the techniques of the Van Eycks or Leonardo.

Once outdoors in the light and sun, these newly liberated paint-

[9] Grosser, *The Painter's Eye,* p. 62.
[10] Grosser, *The Painter's Eye,* pp. 64–66.

ers of the Impressionist school rapidly evolved a startlingly new color theory in keeping with their new, outdoor studio. The painters of the "official" persuasion had worked indoors in studios with the much vaunted north light as sole illumination for their models. North light is cool and even a bit bluish, causing the illuminated areas to appear cool also. The color of the materials and surfaces in a studio is generally warm, resulting in reflected shadows on the model which are also warm. So accustomed were the academic painters to this color system, that even when painting in the sunlight they repeated the formulas of the studio.[11]

The Impressionists reversed this formula. Since sunlight is warm, the bright surfaces of things seen outdoors were painted in bright, warm colors. The blue sky causes the shadows to be bluish and cool. Distances were blued, because the blue color of the air reflecting the blue of the sky creates a cool veil over the landscape. The bright, warm colors were reserved for the foreground, because the sun in nature illuminates the scene in exactly this way. Ironically, the Impressionists reversed the color theory of the academic painters. They insisted upon seeing their interiors as though they were outdoors in the sunlight; blues in shadow areas together with warm highlights are typical of the Impressionist painters. Cézanne's interior compositions are good examples. Vuillard, an anomaly, worked almost entirely indoors, and, in a manner unusual for an Impressionist, made good use of browns and grays. But violet and blue shadows became a trade-mark of the Impressionists, and make possible a simple method for distinguishing their work from all the painters who preceded them.[12]

The portable paint box made possible a variety of schools of painting that flourished from the middle of the nineteenth century to the present day. The "nature" painters created a host of potboilers and a few masterpieces during these years. In the main, however, serious painting has returned to more introspective theories; today few serious painters work outdoors. The elements of design were not emphasized by the outdoor painters, nor were

[11] *Ibid.,* pp. 86–87.
[12] Grosser, *The Painter's Eye,* p. 88.

socially profound themes considered important. The immediate camera-like transcription of the selected theme was the ideal. Like the camera, the Impressionists sought the impersonal, equalized surface tension of the photograph.

The unity of surface is one of the most persistent qualities of modern painting; it allows paintings by such apparently different artists as Andrew Wyeth and Jackson Pollock to be classed together as modern works. The equalized surface of the Impressionists was achieved by means of the application of relatively small, frequently vertical brush strokes. "Monet dabs, Pissarro scatters confetti, Seurat plants polka dots."[13] Jackson Pollock dripped paint until he achieved a tightly knit, unified surface. No center of interest is accented with an extra heavy load of paint as Rembrandt might have done. Andrew Wyeth achieves the same sense of surface unity by hatching and stippling the entire picture until a beautifully fabricated surface is developed. This is a vastly different practice than the method employed by Rembrandt and most of the other old masters; they habitually built up certain areas in heavy impasto, thick layers of paint, and left others flat and smooth. Vermeer is one of the very few painters before the Impressionists whose work is distinguished by an impeccable unity of surface tension. His great recent popularity can be attributed to this quality as well as to his serene and beautifully designed compositions. Van Meegeren, Vermeer's infamous forger, baked his concoctions in an oven in order to achieve the unified surface of a true Vermeer. Some experts believe that Vermeer worked in a similar secret technique; no other painter has ever achieved his special technical qualities.[14]

The great pictures of Vermeer are excellent testimony in support of the theory here proposed: the interrelatedness of form and process in painting. Vermeer's forms appear to be suspended in a bath of light. His edges, or the boundary line between one tone and another, are all equally fused.[15] Whatever his technique, it enabled him to paint form uniquely. Did Vermeer stumble upon his mys-

---

[13] Grosser, *The Painter's Eye,* p. 91.
[14] Grosser, *The Painter's Eye,* p. 57.
[15] *Ibid.,* p. 55.

terious process and then proceed to exploit its advantages? Or did he consciously strive to develop a technique that would give him the forms we know as uniquely Vermeer's? Only Vermeer's testimony appears capable of solving this dilemma; history indicates that either speculation may be correct. The artist's vision may demand a new technique, or the existing technique may control and inspire the artist's vision of new forms.

Although oil painting is still the dominant medium today in the field of fine painting, many artists have attempted to break free of the limitations imposed by the medium. The designs in collage by the Cubists and the eccentric improvisations of the Dada movement are twentieth century examples. Many other artists are experimenting in the hope of discovering a medium that will allow them to express their own unique vision without the danger of repeating the numerous clichés so easily available in the oil medium. Men such as Burri with his wood veneer compositions, Marca-Relli with his heavy canvas collages, and the artists of the recently famous Spanish school who employ synthetic binders with sand in order to create a cement-like effect, are witnesses to the contemporary search for new media. Even those who remain faithful to the oil medium frequently attack the canvas with such violence as to obliterate any resemblance to the traditional technical appearance of the medium.

While they may achieve a new or strikingly different effect, they do not circumvent the old disadvantages of the oil medium in the least. The cracking of many a recently created "Action" painting or Abstract Expressionist design is mute testimony that the technical problems affecting the longevity of the oil paint film have not been solved.

Although it is true that many painters voice the opinion that they would rather paint a good picture that soon falls apart than a bad one that lasts forever, this attitude is not a valid justification for poorly constructed pictures when better means are available. A painter, whatever else he may be, is a craftsman. It is a poor policy to attempt to sell works of art which the artist knows may soon deteriorate; it is, in fact, unethical.

3

Synthetic Painting Media

Although the artist is concerned primarily with the methods and techniques necessary for the proper handling of his materials, it is also important that he have an understanding of the general characteristics and origins of his medium. Such knowledge provides insights requisite to a sensitive solution to esthetic problems. This chapter is designed to provide a rounded view of the entire field of the plastics as it pertains specifically to the new synthetic painting media.

A material is termed "plastic" if it can be softened (frequently by the application of heat) and reformed while in this pliable condition. The newly created form retains its shape by cooling, by the removal of a solvent through evaporation, or by a chemical reaction that renders the plastic infusible. The synthetic painting media, as discussed in this book, do *not* make use of the application of heat; hardening involves either the removing of a solvent or the working of a chemical reaction. The erroneous belief that heat must be applied to the new synthetic painting media has prevented some artists from availing themselves of these versatile materials.

Most of the "plastic" articles sold today are made of either the thermosetting or the thermoplastic variety of the molding plastics. The thermosetting plastics set permanently at a certain temperature and will not soften if reheated. Clay is a familiar example of a thermosetting material; it must be fired in order to retain its shape permanently, and additional heating will not allow reworking of the clay by the potter. The thermoplastics soften with the application of heat. They must be cooled in order to achieve a satisfactory "set." The thermoplastics will resoften if heat is again applied. The metals are classic examples of thermoplastic materials.

In current parlance, the terms "synthetic resin" and "plastics" are synonymous, but not all plastics are synthetic resins. For example, esters and ethers of cellulose, a natural substance, are classed as plastics although they are not synthetic materials. Synthetic resins used in paints and varnishes are commonly not referred to as plastics. A material termed "synthetic" is one which does not occur in nature, but which must be built up in the laboratory. The chemist may create an entirely new material or reproduce a known substance by means of a synthetic process.

The first of the modern synthetic plastics was discovered by a chemist, Dr. Leo H. Baekeland in the year 1901. He found that when he mixed carbolic acid with formaldehyde, a soft, gummy material resulted that nothing would dissolve. After much experimentation, Dr. Baekeland developed a similar substance that could be molded and set by heat; it was named Bakelite in his honor.

Since these early days in the field of the synthetic plastics, chemists have produced and are still producing a bewildering plethora of useful plastics. The painter is hard-pressed to keep up with such a rapidly developing technology. As new materials make their appearance from time to time, it is the responsibility of the concerned painter to evaluate their usefulness to his craft.

All of the modern synthetic plastics are classified as organic substances. This classification is the result of the investigations of early chemists who found that all matter could be classified as either organic or inorganic. Inorganic materials are found in the earth; minerals and metals are good examples. Organic substances appeared to exist only in plant and animal sources. The presence of carbon atoms in a substance is the distinguishing characteristic which separates it from the inorganic materials. Not until about 100 years ago were chemists able to create an organic compound in the laboratory. Creation of this synthetic substance, urea, was soon followed by the development of hundreds of thousands of synthetic, carbon-containing compounds.

Inorganic substances are made of molecules of a relatively simple structure. They contain two, three, or four different kinds of atoms with a low total atomic number per molecule. The inclusion of the carbon atom adds the probability of molecular complexity, resulting in molecules resembling long chains or rings, due to the propensity of the carbon atom to attach itself to other carbon atoms as well as to attract and hold atoms of other elements. Organic molecules and the substances they make up are very sensitive to heat, thus the thermosetting and thermoplastic characteristics of the modern synthetic plastics.

The molecule is the smallest amount of a given substance that still retains all of the characteristics of the parent substance. As the chemist changes the arrangement or structure of molecules, so changes the character of the substance they comprise. The term for the process of forming larger molecules is "polymerization," and the resulting substance is called a "polymer." The two basic methods for forming modern plastic materials are termed condensation polymerization and vinyl (or addition) polymerization. It will be noted that many of the media discussed in this book include the word "vinyl" in their names. The vinyl polymers are outstanding because there are no by-products from the reaction necessary to create them. This property is largely responsible for the modern development of low pressure molded products; no volatile wastes are formed during the molding process.

The ingredient necessary in order to induce polymerization is termed the "catalyst." The term "monomer" is used to indicate a polymer-making substance that has not as yet begun to polymerize. The molecules of the polymer are often gigantic relative to the original monomer; the polymerized molecule may contain thousands of molecules of the original monomer. Not all molecules will polymerize. Chemists refer to molecules that have a tendency to polymerize under certain conditions as a "functional group." A "co-polymer" is one that is built up of more than one kind of molecule. In the literature on the new synthetic media for the painter, the terms defined here are frequently encountered. The artist will find that a reasonable working knowledge of the terms and concepts involved is most helpful.

Polyvinyl acetate, polyvinyl chloride resin, the epoxies and polyesters, and the arcylic resins are products of the chemist's laboratory. All of them have been found especially useful to the painter. The paints derived from the acrylic resins, however, have become the most widely accepted new synthetic media. For example, the Spanish painter, Antoni Tápies, award winner of a recent Carnegie International Exhibition, employs a mixture of marble dust and an acrylic resin polymer emulsion. Hundreds of less famous painters have also abandoned the traditional media for one of the acrylic resin derivatives.

Because of the dominant position of the acrylic resin paints, it will be useful to trace the history, method of formulation, and properties of this excellent synthetic binder. Dr. Otto Rohm, founder of the Rohm and Haas Company, one of the leading producers of acrylic resin products, investigated the possibilities of commercially producing these resins as a substitute for drying oils and lacquers. Although he had begun work in this area as early as 1901, the year his doctoral thesis was published, it was not until 1915 that he was able to secure a patent on the process for commercial production.

After World War II, two synthetic binders dominated the commercial paint field: the butadiene styrene and polyvinyl acetate emulsions. Although vastly superior to commercially available paints at that time, these binders still exhibited tendencies that made them less than ideal. Some of these difficulties included emulsion breakage, lack of freeze resistance, viscosity changes in storage, and putrification and embrittlement during the aging process.[1]

The earlier patented process for the production of acrylic paints proved to be too costly. Fortunately, in 1953, an entirely new process was announced for the production of acrylate monomers. This process was much less expensive than the earlier methods had

[1] Gerould Allyn, *Basic Concepts of Acrylic Emulsion Paint Technology* (Philadelphia: Rohm & Haas Company, 1956), pp. 1-2.

(By permission of Harry E. Hellmuth, Jr.)

Fig. 3 "White Wall." A recent acrylic resin painting by the author. The design is underlaid with paper collage; the wall is underpainted with Magna white. The painting is finished in polymer tempera. Winner of three awards.

been; acrylic resin paints were finally available at competitive prices.

In the formulation of acrylic resin paints, the chemist has a wide choice of useful monomers. Some of these substances are much harder and less flexible than others. By means of a suitable selection of monomers, the chemist can formulate acrylic resins ranging from tough solids to syrupy liquids suitable for painting media. Binders of the polyvinyl acetate type have not had this degree of flexibility of formulation available to the chemist, with the result that their development has lagged.

Acrylic resin emulsions are thus seen to be closely related to the acrylic plastics. Plexiglas and Lucite are the most well-known and time-tested of these exciting new materials. Acrylic binders share with these plastics the properties of exceptional color retention, excellent resistance to water and alkali, and outstanding resistance to deterioration during the aging process.[2]

The most outstanding characteristic of the acrylic resins is their high order of transparency: they are clearer than all but the highest grade of optical glass. This clarity remains as long as the material survives, in contrast to the yellowing and darkening of the traditional oil medium. Acrylic resin paints are also fast drying, a characteristic that is appreciated by most painters. Acrylic resin emulsions are very stable. Freeze-thaw cycles and aging do not affect acrylic resin emulsions; their resistance to coagulation by soluble salts is high, allowing them to be diluted with ordinary tap water. Because of these very desirable and unique characterictics, the various derivatives of acrylic resin have demonstrated their excellence as painting media. Rhoplex AC-33, an excellent acrylic resin emulsion, can be bought in bulk quantities directly from the manufacturer, the Rohm & Haas Company. This medium can be used directly with pigments and other materials; no additives are required or desirable.

Henry Levison, president of Permanent Pigments, Inc., believes that the immediate future will see the development of a number of co-polymers with special advantages for the painter. Permanent

---

[2] Allyn, *Basic Concepts of Acrylic Emulsion Paint Technology,* p. 4.

Pigments, Inc. now has a co-polymer of drying oil and acrylic resin which is used in their rapid-drying Texture White Underpaint. Most of the major producers of artists' paints are experimenting with these promising new combinations.

Mr. Levison has conducted a series of outdoor durability experiments with a variety of organic paints. He notes that the oil medium has a very limited life when exposed to the elements, but that the vinyls, polyvinyls, and acrylics last much longer. When painted on a slab of concrete which was placed in a vertical position facing south, the acrylic emulsion colors remained unimpaired for from two to three years. In from three to four years, the surface had begun to weather and the less permanent colors such as Hansa yellow, ITR naphol, and Indigo orange showed some fading. The areas painted with the commonly used permanent colors were in passable condition. This is probably the limit of durability of the presently available organic binding materials. It is true that automobile finishes or multicoat house paint may last longer, but their films are not as complex as those in fine painting.

House and automobile paints last as long as it takes the weathering process to wear off most of the paint. In fine painting, however, the *beginning* of any appreciable weathering marks the *end* of the life of the painting. Therefore, for exterior durability, the use of glazed ceramic techniques is the only reliable method. If the sun, rain, and snow do not directly strike an outdoor synthetic media painting, however, durability is very great.[3]

Mr. Levison, Mr. Bocour, and the many artists interviewed who now use synthetic media, are all hopeful that these new materials will have a broad future in the field of fine painting. Both the oil and the water-compatible synthetic media have performed successfully. The many advantages of the synthetic media over the traditional media should rapidly encourage their use by most artists. A tour of any contemporary exhibition will convince even the most skeptical that many painters have found the new synthetic media to be superior.

[3] Henry Levison, letter to the author, December 22, 1961.

4

Polymer Tempera

Polymer tempera has become the most popular new medium developing out of recent research in the area of synthetic binders for fine painting. Polymer tempera's range and technical versatility make it unique. This excellent medium has met with success at all levels, from the child in the classroom to the professional painter. Muralists have been especially enthusiastic. Because it is so applicable to a wide variety of painterly techniques, polymer tempera encourages experimentation as no other medium has been able to do. Polymer tempera's ability to incorporate into its paint film ingredients other than the traditional pigments is one of the medium's most unusual characteristics. Expression through the use of the medium is not hampered by dependence on standard manipulations and remembered clichés. Whereas the oil medium or any of the other traditional media must be carefully manipulated for good results, as the chapter on traditional media emphasizes, polymer tempera can be used with almost no thought of inhibiting rules and precautions. Polymer tempera allows one to employ very simple, direct methods or very complex and sophisticated techniques. It is a medium with which to learn and to grow.

The polymer tempera medium is perhaps the closest medium of all the recently developed synthetic binders to the ideal medium, a binder completely without technical problems or flaws. This single synthetic medium may well represent the most significant advance in the long history of the painter's quest for the ideal medium.

Alfred Duca is credited with developing the first polymer tempera medium, a polyvinyl acetate emulsion. He began his experiments in 1945 and worked with the Borden Company to produce a highly polymerized grade of polyvinyl acetate which was also relatively acid-free. (Elmer's Glue is a Borden product made from a polyvinyl acetate base but without the necessary qualities required in a good artist's medium.) Further work led to the selection of a nonmigrating plasticizer that caused the new medium to be suitably transparent and free from embrittlement. Duca has since painted many excellent works in this versatile medium. Additional technical experiments by him have been carried out under Ford and Rockefeller Foundation research grants.

Due to Alfred Duca's generosity, artists may now formulate their own polyvinyl acetate emulsion medium at considerable savings. The following are directions he has made available for this book:

1. Directions for the formulation of 5 gallons:
   To 5 gal. of polyvinyl acetate emulsion (Polyco 953-7 A), add 16 oz. of Resoflex 296 in the following way: Slowly pour the Resoflex 296 into 1 gal. of polyvinyl acetate emulsion while stirring. After complete solution has taken place, add this mixture to the remaining 4 gal. of the polyvinyl acetate emulsion. Next, add 4 oz. of Cellosize, pouring slowly. Finally, dissolve ⅛ oz. of Naconal R.S.F. wetting agent in a small amount of hot water and add to the batch. Allow to stand for 24 hours before using.

2. Directions for the formulation of 55 gallons:
   One drum of Polyco 953-7 A usually contains 55 gallons of material. In order to make this amount of painting medium, take 6 gal. of the Polyco 953-7 A and add 5½ qts. (or 1 gal., 1 qt., 1 pt.) of Resoflex 296. Pouring must be accomplished slowly while stirring. The stirrer (a wood or glass rod) *must* be kept free of Resoflex. Allow this mixture to stand for 24 hours. Add this mixture to the remainder of the

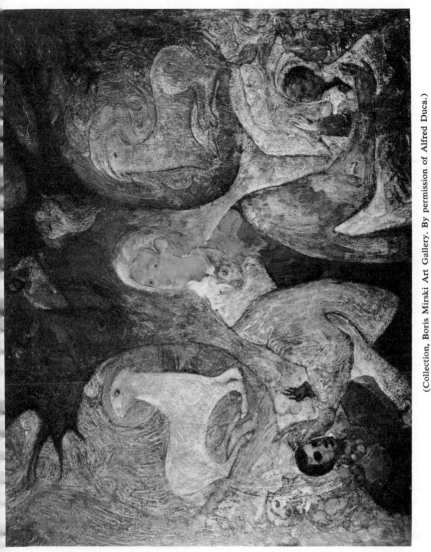

Fig. 4 "Pole Star," by Alfred Duca. A polyvinyl acetate polymer tempera by the discoverer of the medium.

drumful and allow to stand for another 24 hours. Next, dissolve 1⅜ oz. of Naconal R.S.F. wetting agent in a small amount of hot water and add to 5½ cups (or 1 qt., ½ pt., 4 oz.) of Cellosize. Dissolve this mixture by pouring slowly into 5 gal. of the polyvinyl acetate emulsion mixture described above. Stir thoroughly for 15 minutes and then add to the remainder of the batch. Note: In order to prevent coagulation, never dilute polyvinyl acetate polymer tempera with water that is below 40° F.

The above directions will make the polyvinyl acetate polymer tempera medium for about $4.25 per gallon. Suppliers of the materials required are listed in the section "Sources of Materials." It is advisable to write to the manufacturers; they may supply the materials directly or suggest local dealers.

Two distinct media are included under the generic term "polymer tempera." One is the polyvinyl acetate medium described above, while the other is formulated from acrylic resin by at least three manufacturers. Permanent Pigments, Inc., and Bocour Artist Colors, Inc., make their polymer tempera products from a base of Rhoplex AC-33, the Rohm & Haas Company's well-tested acrylic resin emulsion. The products are trade-named Liquitex and Aqua-Tec respectively.

José Gutiérrez, one of the first and ablest experimenters in the field of the synthetic media, markets an excellent acrylic polymer tempera medium, Politec, produced by the Politec Artist Colors Company. It is made in Mexico, but can also be purchased in the United States. (See "Sources of Materials.")

The two media behave very similarly, but there are some important differences. Polyvinyl acetate provides the hardest films, strongest adhesive power, and better development of color with some pigments, particularly the iron oxides. Technical difficulties, however, have prevented any manufacturer from bringing out a line of colors employing a polyvinyl acetate emulsion.

Rhoplex AC-33, on the other hand, appears to have overcome these problems. The above mentioned companies sell an excellent range of prepared polymer tempera colors that have very satisfactory characteristics. Most painters who use polymer tempera make use of the acrylic resin emulsion colors and medium. The directions supplied in this chapter by Alfred Duca may now encourage more painters to work with polyvinyl acetate polymer tempera.

In order to better understand the uniqueness of the polymer tempera media, the following list of characteristics is presented:

1. Polymer tempera is rapid drying. Less than 30 minutes is required for the paint film to become dry to the touch. The humidity level is the controlling factor.
2. It is water-compatible.
3. It is water-resistant upon drying. Overpainting offers no danger of the colors bleeding through from the underpainting.
4. It may be built up to any thickness without concern for durability. Successive layers need not be graded according to thickness.
5. Many otherwise incompatible techniques and manipulations can be combined in one work.
6. The polymer tempera medium is compatible with a variety of colors. Dry pigments, water-dispersed pigments, casein colors, and most paints which have organic gum bases are useful.
7. Inert aggregates such as marble dust, sand, clay, and talc can be employed as well as paper pulp, shredded asbestos, sisal hemp, and many similar inert substances.
8. Polymer tempera paintings can be cleaned with a damp cloth.
9. Polymer tempera paintings are unaffected by light, or moderate heat. They will not crack, yellow, or darken with age. (This applies only if the coloring agents and support are made of quality materials.)
10. The polymer tempera medium is nontoxic, given reasonable use, and noninflammable.

11. Polymer tempera colors need not change color or value on drying if the artist so desires.
12. It will adhere to a wide variety of surfaces.

Because the oil painting medium is the modern standard, it is instructive to compare the listed characteristics of polymer tempera with those of oil. Since the history of the progression from one medium to another has been one in which each succeeding advance has been in the direction of a more versatile binding material, it is not difficult to imagine that new generations of artists will recognize the pronounced superiority of the synthetic binders. The present generation of painters has matured without youthful experimentation in the new synthetics; skill in the traditional media, which was painfully acquired only after countless hours of study and practice, is not readily discarded. Nevertheless, the new media are gaining rapidly in popularity. One of the new synthetic media, polymer tempera perhaps, is very likely to become the new standard.

The following is a detailed comparison of the properties of the polymer tempera and oil media:

1. Rapid drying is usually considered to be a very desirable quality in any medium. Oil is a slow drier and has plagued painters for centuries because of this one difficulty. Certain kinds of blending are possible only if a medium dries slowly, but by and large most painters prefer not to indulge in these rather characterless methods. The point is that one *cannot* get oil to dry rapidly; siccatives which accelerate drying are technically dangerous. Too much will ruin a painting. But even when siccatives are used, oil does not compare in drying time with any of the other traditional media or with the synthetic medium, polymer tempera.

2. The fact that a medium can be thinned with water results in a host of desirable characteristics, especially when compared with thinning by the addition of oil and turpentine. Importantly, water is inexpensive and universally available. Those who find the odor of oils and turpentine unpleasant can have no complaint against polymer tempera. It gives off only the faintest of odors which, un-

like those of oil and turpentine, completely disappears in a matter of minutes. An advantage of no mean importance is the ease with which a water-compatible paint can be washed off clothing and other materials should an accident occur. This is an especially important consideration when paints are employed as instructional materials in classes for the young. Brushes, other painting tools, and palettes are also easily cleaned with water. Should oil colors harden on a rug or article of clothing, removal is exceedingly difficult without permanently damaging the fibers of the material. Should an accident occur while using polymer tempera, the hardened material can be removed with a solvent especially manufactured for this purpose or with a good lacquer thinner. Brushes may also be cleaned in this manner. Special cleaning is unnecessary, however, if the brushes are kept in water when not used for applying paint. Water-base paints are commonly held to be much more manageable than are oil-base paints; polymer tempera partakes of these desirable characteristics.

3. Most water-base paints are difficult to overpaint because of the tendency of the underpainting to bleed through or loosen under the dissolving influence of the watery medium. A water-resistant underpainting, therefore, is a decided advantage to the painter. Once polymer tempera colors have set up, water will not disturb the paint film unless its is immersed and scrubbed. After a few days of drying, even this extreme treatment will not remove the polymer tempera film from a porous support.

Oil paint layers require considerable time to set up if bleeding is not to occur. Some dye colors may bleed through an oil film even after years of drying. Because of the inert nature of the polymer tempera film, problem colors are locked into a homogeneous mass much like glass. The polymer tempera film is not porous as the oil film frequently is, and does not allow the colors to creep from one layer to another. The artist's freedom to glaze and scumble almost immediately after laying in the underpainting is especially helpful. Traditionally, painters in oil have found it necessary to wait for two weeks or more before applying final glazes. This slowness is a decided handicap and accounts for the infrequency with which many contemporary oil painters make use of the richness and depth available through glazing techniques.

The old masters were more patient and were willing to allow a painting to stand until it was sufficiently dry before continuing. Much of today's brutal, insensitive paint quality is due to the difficulty encountered by artists working too rapidly in oil. Even Picasso has painted many of these matte-surfaced, dull passages. To conclude, the polymer tempera medium has a decided advantage over the oil medium on this specific point. Full, rich, paint quality is available to the painter in polymer tempera without the undue delay required by the drying of the underlayers.

4. Overpainting in impasto, or heavily built up layers of paint, is a constant source of difficulty and concern to the painter in oil. Unless a great deal of craft knowledge is brought to bear, the finished picture is almost certain to crack. Recently finished contemporary oil paintings often show signs of incipient deterioration. This unfortunate tendency is due to the development of unequal tensions as layer is piled upon layer. The unequal oil absorption of the various pigments used and the differences in drying time required by differences in layer thickness, account for unequal layer tensions. The importance of painting "fat over lean" is discussed in the section on oil painting. Each succeeding layer must be more flexible than the layer beneath. An oil painting does not dry as a homogeneous mass, but cures layer by layer, at different rates of speed. The wonder is that some oil paintings have been sufficiently well made to withstand the stresses involved. The fact is that the vast majority of oil paintings have suffered varying degrees of decay attributable to this single factor.

Polymer tempera dries as a homogeneous mass; a chemical bond knits each layer to preceding ones. Expansion and contraction occur uniformly. No inter-layer tensions develop. An oil painting may require years to dry completely, whereas a polymer tempera painting is dry within a few hours. Any defects which may develop will show up within this short period. The polymer tempera medium locks in the pigments and other materials that have been used. If one were to enlarge a cross-section of a polymer tempera paint film, one would observe that each pigment particle is isolated from its neighbor, much as a butterfly or grasshopper can be sealed into an ornamental plastic cube. The result is an inert mass displaying no latent tensions with which to threaten the life of the finished work in polymer tempera. The artist may freely pile thin layers over thick, or thick impasto over thin underpainting, with absolutely no concern for permanency. On this specific point, the polymer tempera medium is the equal of the ideal medium discussed in another chapter.

5, 6, 7. These three points can best be discussed together:

The opportunity to combine many otherwise incompatible techniques within the one medium, polymer tempera, is an obvious advantage. A wide variety of painterly effects can be achieved by combining casein colors, watercolors, and dry pigments, as well as any inert material. The use of polymer tempera with pastels and collage is typical of the uses that can be made of the medium in combination with familiar materials. The following is a list of some of the materials that have been used in place of the traditional color pigments: paper pulp, paper, shredded asbestos, textiles, wood flour, plaster of Paris, ground cork, sisal hemp, clay, kaolin, sand, talc, expanded mica, Vermiculite, Perlite, stone, slate, and Fiberglas cloth. These materials may be mixed into the polymer tempera medium and colors for their special effects or textural contributions. They can be built up beyond the sculptural depth of any traditional medium, in fact they can be made so distinctly three-dimensional as to constitute a bas-relief. So substantial is the solidified mass resulting from the welding together of these materials that it is possible to create sculptures with the polymer tempera medium as the binder. That the oil medium would never be able to withstand such usage is obvious. One must be cautioned that oily materials or surfaces are *not* compatible with polymer tempera. Other acrylic resin paints, however, such as Magna colors and Lucite are compatible with oil.

Because of the newness of the polymer tempera medium, few of its technical potentialities have been explored. There is a tendency for experimenters to proceed much as they would with traditional media. This cautious attitude can be found whenever artists discover a new medium with untested possibilities: as described earlier, the first oil painters proceeded much as they had in egg tempera. Although predicting the appearance of future paintings is impossible, there is little doubt that they will be very different from traditional paintings in traditional media. Even now, many contemporary paintings are technically very original. Much more experimentation is sure to follow.

To conclude: Neither oil paint nor any other traditional medium can compare with polymer tempera on this specific point—the compatibility with a great variety of materials as coloring and texturing ingredients.

8. The cleaning of oil paintings as well as the preservation of their surfaces by varnishing has always been a hazardous procedure. Damar varnish, the medium most frequently recommended for the varnishing of oil paintings, will often powder off within fifty years. Even if all has gone well during this period, the painting must then be revarnished. Only pictures under the care of an expert curator are so handled; most of the others quickly deteriorate due to the deleterious effects of moisture and air pollution. The removal of the old varnish before it is entirely useless is the usual procedure. This process is very painstaking, however, and not at all foolproof. No solvent is guaranteed to remove the varnish and dirt while automatically stopping at the surface of the painted layers.

Water is recommended by some authors for the cleaning of oil paintings, but it is hazardous in the extreme. Cracks will quickly absorb sufficient water to attack the painting from behind, loosening it from the support. Solvents such as alcohol have only a mechanical effect on the oil film; water solutions such as soap and mildly alkaline compounds usually involve chemical action. After the varnish has been removed, chemical action can subtly weaken the paint film and alter the color relationships. Most oil paintings exhibit deteriorated areas resulting from faulty restoration procedures. One of the most common defects is the "skinned" painting, one in which a portion of the actual painting has been removed along with the varnish. Since restoration procedures of the kind described here are periodically necessary, few pictures have been able to escape the dangers involved.

Polymer tempera, once it has dried for a few days, is insoluble in water. Cleaning requires none of the dangerous procedures outlined above. One need only wipe the surface of the polymer tempera painting with a damp cloth. A mild soap solution can be used. No other method is necessary or advised. No traditional medium can be cleaned so easily and safely.

9. The ability of the polymer tempera medium to withstand the rigors of light, heat, and a semi-outdoor exposure is one of the most outstanding attributes of this synthetic binder. Polymer tempera is alkali-proof and acid-proof. Traditional media, including oil paint films, are very vulnerable to these destructive agents. There are no examples from the long history of art to encourage a painter to submit his work to the ravages of a semi-outdoor setting. Strong sunlight will fade the oil color film. Valuable oil paintings are always kept away from sunlight, protected by an even temperature, and hung in a nonhumid place.

José Gutiérrez reports that at present 90 per cent of the murals painted in Mexico have been made with his Politec acrylic medium; excellent results have been reported under all kinds of climatic conditions. In the city of Jalapa, in the state of Vera Cruz, one mural was painted in an exposed, exterior location. No changes have taken place since its creation, even though Jalapa is a damp and rainy place.[1] There is every likelihood that architects will increasingly design exteriors with spaces assigned for murals painted in the new synthetic media. Mexico already has a long tradition of outdoor and semi-outdoor mural painting. The implications for the future decoration of public and private buildings are profound.

The fact that polymer tempera will not crack, yellow, or darken with age is an extremely important characteristic of this new medium, as well as its tremendous resistance to abrasion and em-

[1] José Gutiérrez, letter to the author, May 25, 1963.

(Courtesy of the Instituto Nacional de las Bellas Artes, Mexico City.)

Fig. 5 "Liberación," by Jorge Gonzales Camarena. A recent mural by the well-known Mexican artist, painted on canvas with Politec.

brittlement. Cracking is usually attributed to the strain of unequal tensions between layers of paint, but polymer tempera does not have this defect. The paint film is very flexible; polymer tempera paintings, especially those made of acrylic resin, can be rolled in a manner that would permanently damage an oil painting.

The defects of yellowing, cracking, and darkening have plagued curators and painters for centuries. They constitute the principal reason for the deterioration and decay of the world's painted treasures. If the analyses and prognostications of physicists and chemists are accurate, and there is no reason at the present time to question their findings, the new synthetic media will soon give rise to a large number of paintings with great potential for longevity.

Oil paint on canvas is a notoriously impermanent structure; the new media promise to erase the technical problems growing out of this unstable combination of materials. If the support is also a synthetic, as is frequently the case today, longevity is increased even more.

10. Because polymer tempera is noninflammable and nontoxic, it is an ideal medium for use in the classroom. Reasonable use is advised, however; one should not drink the medium or otherwise use it foolishly. Oil and turpentine are inflammable and give off a strong odor. Many find this odor very pleasant, a nostalgic impetus to dreams of centuries of busy artists. Others, however, are sickened by the fumes. Any teacher can tell of students who were not able to remain very long in a room crowded with energetic users of these media. Romance aside, most painters are just as happy not to breathe too much of these fumes; even the hardy find that long hours of exposure dull the senses. The most harmless volatile solution should not be allowed to fill the air of a poorly ventilated room continuously, because of the fire risk and the danger to health. The oil painter sometimes finds uses for highly volatile materials like gasoline, benzol, and acetone. These materials are certainly not appropriate for the classroom.

Certain commercial watercolor and tempera paints are also toxic, depending on the dyes and pigments used. Emerald green, Naples yellow, chrome yellow, cremnitz white, cobalt violet, and all the lead colors should be handled with care. Because there is often a considerable amount of arsenic in dark watercolors, one must be careful not to put the brush in one's mouth as may happen in a moment of absentmindedness.

The nontoxicity of the polymer tempera medium offers a distinct advantage for the user as well as for the responsible teacher. Neither need be concerned about the handling of these synthetic materials; all one's energies can be directed to the painterly problems at hand, without time consuming precautions and worrisome taboos. Polymer tempera, then, is again found to have an advantage over traditional media and to approach the standards of the ideal painter's medium.

11. A most annoying and distracting characteristic of water-soluble paints is the tendency of colors and values to change as the medium dries. Some temperas darken, but most become considerably lighter. This tonal changeability is especially unfortunate in the darker colors and values, destroying depth and richness. Fresco lightens, egg tempera lightens, and so do watercolors. The effect is least annoying when watercolor is painted on white paper, allowing the paper to stand for the white areas. In this case, the brilliance of the paper causes the dark passages to appear properly dark by contrast. Unless a water-soluble medium is varnished, it is impossible to achieve much richness.

The effect of uneven drying on the finished picture is one problem, but to the artist as he works from relationship to relationship, the changing of values and colors during the drying process is a decided disadvantage. The artist finds that he cannot match one tone with another; the usual method employed to circumvent this problem is to mix enough paint of a particular hue so that a new mixture will not be necessary. Only flat, simple passages can be so handled. It is a technique better suited to simple effects in commercial art than to the subtleties of fine painting. Even commercial illustrators complain about the frustration of working in a medium that constantly shifts in tone. One of the reasons for the great popularity of the oil medium among artists is the fact that oil colors do not change markedly from the wet to the dry state. Polymer tempera is unique among water-compatible paints in that it possesses this desirable characteristic of oil paint. Polymer tempera again is seen to approximate the ideal painting medium.

12. One of the most important and unique advantages of polymer tempera is its ability to adhere to a wide variety of surfaces such as paper, wallboard, wood, Masonite, stucco, masonry, plaster, cardboard, stone, and canvas. Any surface that is not greasy or oily will do. Excessively nonporous or slick surfaces should also be avoided. The tenaciousness of polymer tempera allows the painter the use of a wide range of textured supports for his work. Materials commonly used in building construction are frequently ideal, permitting the artist to execute murals without elaborate preparation. He is also freed from restrictions on his time and his inventiveness imposed by the care that must be taken to insure adequate results in other, traditional media. Oil paintings, if properly constructed, must be supported by carefully formulated grounds; frescos are possible only on plaster; watercolor paintings require paper; and egg tempera necessitates the most carefully prepared gesso ground.

Polymer tempera has a clear advantage here. Except for the fact that it will not adhere to oily surfaces, polymer tempera is very close to the ideal painting medium.

Of the twelve characteristics of polymer tempera listed above, only the eleventh one is equaled by the oil medium. In order to be objective in making these comparisons, one must also compare polymer tempera with oil on the basis of oil's characteristics and advantages. These are listed on page 24. The following is a short discussion of the items on this list and their relationship to the preceding discussion of the qualities of polymer tempera:

1. The oil medium offers a wide range of effects compared to traditional media, but we have seen how polymer tempera offers a far greater range of effects as discussed under items 4, 5, 6, 7 and 12 in this chapter.

2. The use of oil as opaque and transparent paint films in the same painting is surpassed by polymer tempera as discussed under items 3 and 4 above.

3. Oil color's property of remaining unchanged from the wet to

the dry state is equaled by polymer tempera, as discussed under item 11 above.

4. The flexibility of the oil paint film, enabling large paintings to be rolled and easily transported is surpassed by the greater flexibility of the polymer tempera paint film. When rolling polymer tempera, however, one should be cautioned against working in temparatures colder than about 70 degrees. Polymer tempera is less flexible when cold and may crack if violently rolled, twisted, or bent when chilled.

5. The oil medium is slow drying, but this characteristic is not considered to be an advantage by most contemporary painters.

6. The universal acceptance of the oil medium by artists and public alike is the single advantage it has over polymer tempera. Until the new synthetic media have been in use for a considerable period of time and have gained the confidence of all concerned, there is little likelihood that the oil medium will be seriously challenged on this point. The rise of science and the favorable judgments by men of science may accelerate acceptance. Although the public is now almost totally ignorant of the rapid development of the synthetic painting media, the same cannot be said of the painters. More and more of them are adopting synthetics in lieu of the traditional media, as has been noted.

This chapter has sought to demonstrate that polymer tempera is a medium of remarkable characteristics. This one synthetic medium alone has sufficient advantage over the traditional media to make polymer tempera today as revolutionary a medium as oil once was.

5

Polymer Tempera Techniques

An impressive literature dealing with the techniques of fine painting has long been available for the education of the serious student. From Cennini and Vasari to Doerner and Mayer, one can trace the artist's efforts to understand and control his technical means. The new synthetic media must now be given the same exhaustive attention as the traditional media have received. The Artists Technical Research Institute, Inc. (240 East 20th Street, New York 3, N.Y.) is researching technical problems and media, both new and old. The Institute is directed by Ralph Mayer. A journal is planned in which the Institute's findings will be made available together with articles of value on the training of artists and matters of interest to the practicing painter. At present, however, there is very little instructional material in the new media available.

Alfred Duca has graciously made his *Polymer Tempera Handbook* available as a source work for this chapter. His wide experience in the teaching of children and serious artists has resulted in an unequaled reservoir of useful information.

The purpose of this chapter is to supply the most complete information available today on the subject of the techniques employable by one who works with polymer tempera; the preceding chapter supplied the information necessary for an understanding of the technical resources of the medium.

61

Although the use of polymer tempera necessitates few technical restrictions or precautions, there are some suggestions that can prove helpful.

Storage When storing or mixing the polymer medium, glass containers are best. Avoid tin, iron, or galvanized metal; they will discolor the medium or any admixture with pigments. The medium can be stored indefinitely in tightly sealed jars. In the case of polyvinyl acetate emulsions, temperatures should not be extreme. If frozen, the polyvinyl acetate medium will coagulate irreversibly. When the polyvinyl acetate medium is mixed with dry pigments, caseins, watercolors, and other compatible media, storage should be limited to three weeks.

Hand Care Although the polymer medium is nontoxic, sensitive skins may be irritated by prolonged immersion or contact with polymer tempera mixtures. The average individual however, will find this warning unnecessary. Water and soap easily wash the medium from the hands.

Brushes Standard bristle, camel's hair, or sable brushes can be used, but nylon brushes last longest. Always wet the brush in water before dipping it into a polymer tempera mixture. One must be careful not to allow the medium to dry on the brush.

The artist will find that three or more brushes are useful while working on a painting; those not immediately in use can be soaking in a container of water. At the end of a painting session, the brushes should be cleaned thoroughly with soap and *cold* water. Lestoil is useful. A brush cleaner and solvent is available from the producers of polymer tempera or lacquer thinner may be used; hardened paint can thus be removed from brushes or clothing. Brushes can also be cleaned by soaking them overnight in acetone or methyl alcohol. One must be careful with these solvents, however, due to their inflammable and toxic fumes.

Palettes A smooth, nonabsorbent surface makes the best polymer tempera palette. Glass, Plexiglas, and enamel are excellent for this purpose. Palettes may be cleaned by immersion in water for an hour, or by allowing wet newspaper to soak on the palette overnight. In either case the polymer tempera film will readily peel off.

Test Mixtures Although polyvinyl acetate polymer tempera is compatible with most aqueous paints, test mixtures should be made before an important work is undertaken. Some colors contain borax which will coagulate the medium immediately.

Supports for polymer tempera paintings can be made of any material that is not greasy or oily. Most painters, however, still prefer to work on canvas, Masonite panels, or illustration board. A polymer tempera gesso is available from the paint producers. This product is especially useful if a white ground is desired. Traditional gessos may be used, but the new polymer tempera gessos are stronger, more flexible, and more easily prepared. The polymer medium and colors may be applied directly to the unsized canvas with no danger of the cloth fiber deteriorating as would be the case if oils were used. Untempered Masonite should be lightly sanded in order to remove the water-repellent finish. Mayer and others caution against the use of tempered Masonite because of the oily substance with which it is impregnated.

An interesting new synthetic base gesso developed by Charles Seide of Cooper Union is "Museum Quick-On Gesso." This brilliant white ground will adhere to tempered Masonite as well as to oily or shiny surfaces such as old oil paintings. The Charles Seide gesso and the polymer tempera varieties will not deteriorate in liquid form, unlike the animal glue binders traditionally used in the formulation of gessos. They offer no storage problem and do not need to be made into a fresh preparation for each application.

Traditionally, the ground was isolated from subsequent paint layers by means of a coat of varnish. This practice is not desirable in the new media. The overpainting in polymer tempera will fuse with the polymer gesso ground, a very important advantage from the standpoint of the longevity of the finished work.

A useful fixative for pastels or drawings can also be made from the polymer tempera medium, thinned with water. The recommended proportion is one part medium to three parts water, but if the liquid will not spray freely from an atomizer, more water can be added.

Children's paintings in poster colors or drawing inks can be made insoluble when dry by the addition of small amounts of polymer tempera medium. This technique can be of great importance to the teacher as well as to the student. Color muddying and bleeding are eliminated, a major hazard in poster painting by children. In addition, the finished painting will not chalk off. By the simple addition of pigments, clays, paper, etc., polymer tempera mixtures can be made which simulate more complex media. Thus the esthetic effects of the oil and watercolor methods can be understood without encountering the technical hazards usually associated with these media. As the young artist matures, he may come to realize that he is working in a medium of vastly greater range than either of these traditional media, and may develop new technical means for his personal expression.

A very useful product that can be used in combination with acrylic resin polymer tempera colors and medium is Liquitex Modeling Paste and Extender sold by Permanent Pigments, Inc. José Gutiérrez markets a similar product, Plastilita, made for use with his Politec colors. This material is an acrylic resin emulsion combined with ground marble to form a finely textured, white paste. It can be used as an extender as well as enabling the artist to work up thick, buttery, paint layers for impasto effects. This material also makes ideal grounds. It can be overpainted with oil, casein, tempera, or polymer tempera paints.

When used on a solid support such as Masonite, such a paste can be built up to the bas-relief level and beyond. Before the medium and admixture has completely set, the surface can be molded and textured with clay modeling or other tools; when completely dry the surface can be worked with knives, chisels, saws, or any edged tool. Antoni Tápies cuts back into his acrylic resin and marble dust bas-relief surfaces in exactly this manner. The material will cut smoothly without chipping and is remarkably resistant to shock and breakage.

A very satisfactory method for texturing a ground made of these materials is to press burlap or any preferred material against the prepared ground before it has dried completely. The texturing material is then removed immediately, creating a negative impression of the material on the ground. Others prefer to leave the material attached, building upon it in collage or in the traditional manner. Another variation can be achieved by stretching muslin or other material over Masonite or plywood, after first coating the board with a solution of one part polymer tempera medium to one part water. Another coat of medium and water brushed over the material will insure a good bond.

Definite proportions of the polymer tempera medium to colors and other incorporated materials are not necessary. The possible variations are great. If there is any concern for the strength of the bond, one need only scratch the surface of the doubtful area. More medium is indicated if the film powders when scratched or rubbed. Most artists tend to use an abundance of medium, although it can be used when diluted to about three parts water and one part medium. Rich mixtures build a thicker tactile quality in the paint surface, a quality most painters prefer. Should a high gloss be desired, large proportions of medium will accomplish this end. As more water is added to the medium, the paint film will appear "flatter" or more matte. Permanent Pigments, Inc. now offers a matte varnish for artists who prefer to decide on the surface qualities of their paintings after they are completed, rather than inhibit creativity during the painting process by an over-concern with technical problems. This very satisfactory varnish is made of an acrylic resin and wax emulsion, and its use removes shiny or dull areas and provides a uniformly soft, wax finish. The artist must be careful not to attempt to paint *over* this varnish, however, because the wax prevents subsequent layers from bonding properly to the underpainting. A matte medium is also available from Permanent Pigments, Inc. for those who desire a very dry, flat finish. This medium can be very useful for certain effects, such as watercolor or tempera characteristics. The matte medium is flatted with colloidal silica. Its only technical drawback is a tendency for the silica to remain cloudy when dry.

If the finished painting does not have as high a gloss as desired, the artist may apply several coats of undiluted medium to the surface with a brush. A more unusual effect can be achieved by pouring the medium directly onto the surface of the painting. The paint-ing must be supported horizontally and diked with plasticine clay or strips of cardboard attached to the edges. Should bubbles form, they may be pierced or sucked up with an eyedropper. After this heavy film has set (it may be as thick as one eighth to one quarter of an inch), a heat lamp may be used to accelerate drying and to improve the gloss and transparency of the film. If cloudy areas persist after painting or pouring the heavy final coats, continued application of the heat lamp will remove the troublesome whitish-ness.

When using polyvinyl acetate polymer tempera, increased trans-parency can be achieved by wetting each successive coat with alcohol, including the final coat. (Gold leaf can be set into the sur-face at this time for excellent effects.) A chemical reaction occurs which is caused by a flex of the resins, creating a permanent fix that will not dull with time. This glossy surface may be further enhanced by polishing with a soft cloth when completely dry. A hard furni-ture wax can be used to obtain a maximum gloss.

Most painters do not care for a finish that resembles lacquer in its high, reflective sheen. Andrew Wyeth does not varnish his egg tempera paintings, preferring a dusty, matte surface. He believes that a high gloss cheapens a picture. Matte finishes, however, are particularly vulnerable to the effects of air pollution and humidity. They may even become mildewed. For most painters, therefore, a balance is desirable: enough varnish to protect the painting, but not enough to make the gloss excessive.

A great many possibilities are available to the painter in polymer tempera that have not been thoroughly explored. The following sug-gestions should prove stimulating to the painter or teacher who wishes to free himself from the esthetic restrictions imposed by traditional technical solutions.

Papier-Mâché   Papier-mâché has long been associated with children's sculptures and puppets. Now, because of the strength of the polymer tempera medium, very permanent structures can be created. These papier-mâché constructions can be used as grounds for painting or as sculpture. To make polymer papier-mâché, soak newspaper or paper toweling in water for two days. Pour off the water and add the desired amount of the polymer tempera medium. If an insufficient amount of the medium is used, the papier-mâché will have little structural strength. A test piece will help the artist to learn how much medium is necessary for his particular paper mixture. Sand and other fine aggregates may be added at this time to aid in the development of texture.

The wet, pulpy mass can be spread over Masonite as the ground for painting, or it can be worked over a frame of wood, wire mesh, Styrofoam, or any of a number of appropriate supports. Styrofoam and wood require a sizing of the medium diluted with an equal part of water. If the developing form is markedly three-dimensional, long strips of paper dipped in the same 50 per cent mixture of tempera medium and water may be wrapped around or woven over the surface. Fine detail can be built up with shredded paper and the polymer tempera medium. If the finished piece is to be a sculpture, it may be painted and textured to meet the artist's requirements; if it is a support for a painting, it may be completed in any of the many ways described in this book.

Monoprinting The monoprinting process requires that the artist transfer a painted image from a nonabsorbent surface such as glass or enamel to an absorbent surface such as paper or cardboard, by means of contact and pressure. As the term "monoprint" implies, only one print is made from each original painting. This simple process is especially useful in classes for children.

Before making the transfer from the glass to the paper, the paper may be sized with a solution of polymer tempera medium, colored or clear. During hot, dry weather, it is helpful to use more water because of the increased rate of evaporation.

The monoprinting process can be used in conjunction with painting for many useful effects. Designs and colors may be worked out on a flexible, nonabsorbent surface such as oilcloth or paper glazed with the polymer tempera medium. When the image is satisfactory, the moist surface can then be pressed against the unfinished painting, transferring the image from the oilcloth or paper. Willem deKooning has transferred images from newsprint to his painted canvases in a similar manner. This very simple and direct printing method has not been thoroughly explored as a technique for painting.

Paper Collage Paper is becoming increasingly popular with painters who wish to take advantage of the unique edges available through tearing and cutting, as well as the rapidity with which designs can be built up and modified in paper collage. The unusual colors and textures of paper are also attractive to artists. Collages by Matisse which exploit the brilliance and crispness of line that no other material could quite equal have been shown in the Museum of Modern Art, in New York City. Other painters, such as Rico Lebrun, use paper in the early stages of their work in order to be able to experiment rapidly with many different design solutions. Mondrian used paper and tape in this manner, carefully tracing off the outline of the finally resolved balance of colors, lines, and shapes. Marca-Relli cuts his shapes from canvas, colors them, and then tentatively shifts the shapes about until his conception is realized. The pieces are then permanently attached to the ground with a polyvinyl acetate glue, such as Elmer's Glue, the same commercial product from which polyvinyl acetate polymer tempera was developed by Alfred Duca. The polymer medium, however, is a much better glue for the serious artist who values permanence.

Most colors used on commercially available papers are highly fugitive. Color Aid and Color Vue papers, much employed by commercial artists, are perhaps the least dangerous for permanent work. The color on the surface of the Color Aid papers is applied in a thick layer in the manner of silk-screen printing. The Color Vue papers are printed from plates.

The best solution to the problem set by the artist's need for a permanently colored paper is the making of one's own collection of colored papers. Matisse mixed his own colors and had them brushed onto large sheets of paper. Oil paints are not suitable for this purpose; the turpentine and oil tend to deteriorate the paper. Polymer tempera colors, however, are ideal. The paint has a very low acid level and the transparent films produce safe, clear colors. Permanent dyes and waterproof inks of guaranteed permanency may also be used in conjunction with the polymer tempera medium.

Once the papers have been locked within the solid, homogeneous mass created by the polymer tempera medium, the great permanency of the binder should impart this quality to the colored papers.

Polymer Tempera Tiles Because polymer tempera can be poured, mosaic tiles can be made in the following manner.

The polymer tempera medium should be mixed with sufficient cement to make a loose, workable paste. Mosaic tiles can be made individually, or a sheet of polymer tempera and cement can be poured into a box which has been lined with a nonabsorbent material, such as Saran Wrap. After the sheet has set for a day or two, it may be carved into the desired shapes and sizes with the aid of a saw or serrated knife. The tiles may then be dipped into a polymer cement mixture of any color. If a high gloss is desired, the tiles may be painted with the polymer tempera medium. Colors may also be added in glazing and scumbling techniques for unusual effects.

The fact that the common binder for these materials is the polymer tempera medium makes it possible to fasten the tiles to any absorbent surface with a coating of polymer tempera medium as the adhesive. A chemical bond creates a single mass of tiles and support.

Although the tiles can be used in the ordinary manner for table tops, trays, etc., they can also be fastened to a rigid support like Masonite, and employed as the ground for a painting. Very unusual and interesting surfaces can be built up in this manner. Mosaic murals, either interior or exterior, can be constructed of these highly durable tiles.

Polymer Tempera Transparencies The polymer tempera medium and colors may be used to make transparencies that closely resemble stained glass. They may be made with the equipment and the techniques described in the preceding section on mosaic tiles. The essential difference between the two kinds of plastic pieces is that one is opaque while the other is transparent or translucent. Rather than mixing cement with the medium, the transparent pieces are made by adding only ink, dyes, and watercolors. Translucent panes can be made by adding casein or poster paint. These pieces of colored plastic can be built up on a white or tinted ground creating another mosaic technique, or they can be assembled in the manner of stained glass. Mobiles may also be designed using polymer tempera transparencies for the colored areas. The following is a description of some of the techniques available to the artist or teacher who may wish to work in this medium.

The colored, but otherwise undiluted polymer tempera medium is poured into small boxes shaped as desired or onto a nonabsorbent flat surface. The artist will find that making a few experimental tiles before working on the final design will be helpful; the whitish cast of colors mixed with the polymer tempera medium may change in appearance when dry. Drying time ranges from four to six hours, depending upon the thickness of the poured layer of medium and upon the degree of humidity present.

Large sheets of colored polymer tempera can be poured for subsequent use as glazes over selected areas of a polymer tempera painting. The great advantage of this method over traditional glazing procedures is that many tints and transparent effects can be experimented with until the painter has achieved the most satisfactory combination. The glazing sheets will adhere easily to the painting surface if there is a thin coating of the medium on the back of the sheet and on the surface of the painting. Gentle pressure or rubbing on the surface of the glazing sheet will complete the bond. An entire painting can be built up in this manner.

If the artist wishes to take full advantage of the transparent panes, he can build designs in such a way as to allow light to come through from the back. These designs can be hung so that the image may be seen from either side. The method for constructing a two-sided painting or mural is simple.

The artist must first lay out his design, full scale, on a flat, horizontal surface. Next the design must be covered with a transparent and nonabsorbent sheet such as Saran Wrap or cellophane. Other transparent materials can be made impervious to the penetration of water and polymer tempera by a thin application of wax, vaseline, or oil. The artist will probably want to separate some of his colors from others in the manner of stained glass. This can be accomplished by building small dikes between the separate areas. Material for the dikes can be made of plasticine clay or a putty made of the polymer tempera medium, pigment, and plaster of Paris that has been well kneaded. The plasticine clay or the putty must be rolled with a rolling pin to a thickness of from one-sixteenth of an inch to one-eighth of an inch. Talcum powder is very useful in preventing the moist clay or putty from sticking to the hands, rolling pin, or rolling board. When the clay or putty sheet is dry to the touch, cut strips of the desired width to be used as the dikes. A metal straight-edge will facilitate accurate cutting. The width and color of these strips will be an important factor in the appearance of the finished work.

Transparent dikes can be made by pouring a sheet of clear polymer tempera medium. When dry, this flat sheet can be cut as described above and fastened to the support with polymer tempera medium. If the strips are thin enough, they may be set on edge, completely eliminating the effect of stained glass lead dividers.

The strips to be used as dikes may be heated with a heat lamp in order to facilitate twisting and bending. If a light coating of the polymer tempera medium will not temporarily hold the dikes in place, pins and staples may be used. After the dikes have been satisfactorily arranged, seal the entire design together with a liberal coating of the polymer tempera medium brushed over all the joints and points of contact with the nonabsorbent covering sheet. The artist must be careful that no holes exist in the dikes, in order to prevent color bleeding as the sections are poured. When the dikes are sealed and dry, pour the desired colors mixed with the polymer tempera medium into the proper areas. If air bubbles appear, they may be pricked or sucked up with an eye dropper.

When the entire mass has dried, remove the pins and staples from the dikes, cover the design with a board, and turn over the design and transparent sheet. A piece of illustration or Bristol board can be slipped between the transparent sheet and the drawing in order to aid in turning over the design. Gently peel away the transparent sheet. If there appear to be wet spots on this underside, be careful that the colors do not bleed. Additional drying time should be allowed. The design may now be lifted carefully by one edge and viewed against the light. An illumination table is useful. Touching-up may be accomplished with the polymer tempera medium and the desired colors, or elaborate glazes and scumbles may be built up.

The finished design is now ready for mounting. For children's work, glass is adequate and inexpensive. For more serious work, sheets of Plexiglas or Lucite make ideal supports. Unlike glass, their expansion and contraction rates are exactly the same as those of the polymer tempera medium and colors. Since both the medium and the support are derived from an acrylic resin (if Liquitex, Aqua-Tec, or Politec is used), they are perfectly compatible.

If glass is to be used as the support, it must be thoroughly cleaned with warm water and soap. A scrubbing with alcohol will remove any unwanted moisture. The glass can be improved as a surface by sanding or scratching it in order to improve the tooth. The artist may then coat the surface of the roughened glass with an undiluted solution of the polymer tempera medium. Allow it to dry. A heating lamp will hasten the drying time and improve the bond. Next, coat the back of the polymer pane with the undiluted polymer tempera medium, and allow this application to become tacky. Carefully press the tacky side against the prepared glass, applying even pressure. The heat lamp may again be used. Under normal conditions of temperature and humidity, the bond should be accomplished within two or three days.

Plexiglas and Lucite not only expand and contract at the same rates as does the dry polymer tempera film, they also have a common solvent, acetone. In order to join the finished polymer tempera pane to the Plexiglas or Lucite support, the artist needs only to brush acetone on the two surfaces to be joined, pressing them together immediately. One must be careful to work in a well ventilated space and avoid an open flame; acetone is highly inflammable. Weight should be applied evenly in order to insure a firm bond.

Rather than pour the colors into separated areas as described above, the artist can achieve similar results by pouring a number of sheets of different colors. When dry, the sheets may be cut and shaped to fit the predetermined plan. The poured method, as opposed to the pre-cut method, allows for an easier achievement of very tight seams. If great detail is desired, however, the pre-cut method is the best because it may be easier to cut the small shapes than to build many dikes. The esthetic effect of the dikes or simulated "leaded" areas can be emphasized or eliminated in either method. Adhesion to a support can be accomplished by either of the two methods described above.

The Brooklyn Polytechnic Institute, in 1958, commissioned the muralist, Abraham Joel Tobias, to construct two large murals for the entrance to a new building. The murals are built on 3' x 10' pieces of ¼" Plexiglas, and overlaid with transparent colored pieces precisely cut to the curves and angles of the design. The murals are both exterior and interior, in the manner of a stained glass window, and develop their impact by means of the passage of light through the design. Duplicate designs were built up on either side of the acrylic base sheet, creating a three-dimensional appearance and adding to the subtlety of the colors when seen from the inside or the outside. As many as six layers were built up in some areas. The completed murals were framed in aluminum and covered on both sides by protective shields of transparent acrylic plastic.[1] This Brooklyn Polytechnic Institute mural is very similar to the paintings that can be made by means of the process described in this section. There is every likelihood that artists of the near future will employ variations of these procedures in the creation of murals for the home as well as for public buildings. The possibilities and opportunities afforded by these new techniques are now almost completely unexplored.

Polymer Tempera Glazing An interesting application of the polymer tempera medium for classroom use is the simulated fire glazing of pottery pieces. The polymer tempera medium can be used to produce a high sheen, closely resembling a fired glaze. The finish is water-resistant, but is not recommended for other than decorative purposes. The teacher may find this application of the

[1] "Murals of Acrylic Plastic Introduce New Art Technique," *Architectural Record,* CXXIV, No. 3 (Sept. 1958), 272.

(Permission of Alfred Duca)
Fig. 6 "King David," by Alfred Duca. A recent sculpture in polyvinyl acetate polymer cement. This work has a beautifully textured, stone-like appearance.

polymer tempera medium ideal for young children, however, enabling them to create the esthetic effect of the authentically fired pot or ceramic sculpture.

Polymer Tempera Cements The polymer tempera medium can be mixed with a variety of aggregates to form cements that are far more durable and workable than the traditional materials. This use of the polymer tempera medium may be as significant a development for the painter as any of the preceding uses discussed in this chapter. The cement mixtures can be employed as heavily textured grounds for painting or the mixtures can be built up as bas-relief or three-dimensional forms. Unlike other cements, additional layers can be added to the previously set layers; the polymer tempera medium creates a chemical bond between the under and over layers. These cements can be cast or built up in a technique similar to that employed in clay modeling. The finished piece can be sanded, chiseled, or buffed. Surface textures of great variety are possible by means of the introduction of a wide range of inert materials. Any desired color can be added to the mixture, or the finished piece can be painted with the polymer medium and colors.

Large sculptural forms require braces and armatures for support. Wood, brass, steel, and copper are suitable materials for this purpose. Iron, tin, or galvanized metal will discolor the polymer tempera medium. Heavy forms should be built up in layers, allowing each to set before continuing. When applying a new mixture to a relatively dry area, dampen the dry area. This procedure will prevent the absorption of the polymer tempera medium by the porous under layers.

If the mural or sculpture is to be exhibited outside, the proportion of polymer tempera medium to cement should not exceed 25 per cent. Aggregates should be added as recommended by the manufacturers for the particular cement employed. The water content will depend on the absorbency of the aggregates used.

The following is a useful, standard mixture: four parts dry cement; one part polymer tempera medium; aggregates and water as required. Combine the cement and aggregates in their dry state. Mix the medium and water in a separate container, and then add to the dry ingredients. More water may be added if the mixture is too stiff and unworkable; the mixture should be resilient and putty-like. If the cohesiveness of the mixture is not adequate to the manipulations desired, the addition of sawdust, flour, or other fibrous materials will help create a workable consistency. To apply heavy mixes to the previously set work, roughen the area to be covered with a wire brush or chisel and undercut for extra grip. Absorbent surfaces may be sized with a solution of one part polymer tempera medium and four parts water, otherwise the polymer tempera medium may be absorbed out of the fresh application. Delayed setting can be achieved by reducing the amount of cement in the mixture and sprinkling in the balance as the work progresses.

Although the polymer tempera cement mixes set quickly, they do not attain maximum strength for many weeks. This very slow curing process results in a greater degree of crystallization and strength than is the case with pure cement mixes. During dry, hot weather it is sound practice to drape a damp cloth over the work in order to extend the drying period, thereby adding even greater strength. If carving or other exacting surface treatment is desired, the work should be done during this initial curing period, approximately the first five days.

In order to increase the strength of the final polymer tempera coat or to add a surface color, the artist should dip, spray, or brush the work with a solution of the polymer tempera medium thinned with water. A diluted solution is necessary in order to insure maximum penetration. Allow this coat to dry, then add several more applications of the same diluted mixture until the surface shows a slight gloss. Color may be incorporated at this time.

Outdoor exposure of the pure polymer tempera medium and colors is not recommended. The reasons for this are discussed in Chapter III, Synthetic Painting Media. With the addition of cement and aggregates, however, a material of great outdoor durability results. Paintings, murals, or sculptures made of this material should weather as well as do many stones. The thickness of the materials must be such that weathering will remove only a small proportion of the design. Colors should be deep into the material if they are to survive any appreciable weathering. These considerations hold true for any material that must survive outdoor exposure.

Polymer Tempera Watercolor Techniques Polymer tempera can be used very effectively in a technique that is similar to watercolor painting. The polymer tempera medium and colors can be thinned to the same consistency of watercolor and applied with the same variety of techniques. Unlike traditional watercolor, however, errors can be corrected in a most ingenious and texturally beautiful manner.

Simply cut or tear pieces of the watercolor paper into appropriate shapes and fasten them over the parts of the painting that are to

(By permission of the Springfield Art Museum, Springfield, Missouri.)

Fig. 7 "Naushon Island." A recent polymer tempera by the author. The beach at the left is made of sand. Other portions are underlaid with paper collage. Winner of two awards.

be repainted. The polymer tempera medium, of course, is used as the adhesive. The best method for accomplishing this is to liberally apply the polymer tempera medium to the back of the paper to be fastened as well as to the area to be covered. An infinite variety of papers may be employed in this process, not merely watercolor paper. Pieces of illustration board with straight edges are useful for flattening out the newly adhered paper and for squeezing the excess polymer medium from underneath the paper. Color may also be effectively applied in this manner, scraping the edge of the illustration board over the surface in a great variety of movements and effects. Some artists use razor blades in the same technique. Illustration board is especially useful, however, because it can be cut to fit the particular passage the artist wishes to paint.

This method can be continued indefinitely. Any thickness is feasible. The painting will always appear as fresh as the first passages because the ground and the underpainting can be continually covered and remade. The artist may also add pieces of paper that are left unpainted for a variety of crisp and excellent effects. Illustration board and Masonite make the best supports for this kind of painting.

Grounds for Polymer Tempera Murals   Should the artist wish to paint a mural on a wall of brick, masonry, or cement block, a suitable ground coat must be applied for enduring results. José Gutiérrez suggests the following.

After cleaning the surface and ascertaining that the wall does not contain any moisture, lightly tap the area to be painted with a pointed hammer or chisel, creating small pock marks and a roughened surface. Next, dust or other particles should be broomed off and the wall dampened well all over, in readiness for the first ground coat. A good mixture is two parts marble dust (medium or number 2), one part gray or white cement, and one-fifth part by volume of hydrated lime. This material is then dry mixed together with small pieces of coconut hair, mane, twine fibers, or similar binding matter. Add water to the mixture and apply to the wall with a trowel.

The application of the first coat can be made freely in order that the final ground coat will adhere well. When the first ground coat is set and dry, dampen it again and apply the final ground coat. This mixture should be made of two parts marble dust (number 1 or 0), one part cement, and one-fifth part by volume of hydrated lime. For best results, Gutiérrez advises that all of this material be dry stirred, then mixed with one-tenth part by volume of Celite #289, before adding water. This mixture provides more plasticity, allowing the final coat to be applied more smoothly. A mason's trowel should be used and the surface left grainy, like smooth sandpaper. When this coat has dried, a sealer should be applied. Gutiérrez advises using his Barniz Sellador, but the polymer tempera medium may be used if other than Politec colors are to be employed in the polymer tempera technique.

Walls made of lime plaster or plaster of Paris require only a sealer, but greater permanency can be achieved by applying the grounds as described above.

The foregoing technical suggestions are necessarily limited. There is every likelihood that many more uses and applications of the polymer tempera medium and colors will be developed. The newness of the medium explains its present underdevelopment.

6

Oil-Compatible, Acrylic Resin Paints

One of the most popular synthetic media on the market today is a new paint from Bocour Artist Colors, Inc., trade-named Magna. This versatile medium is made of acrylic resin dissolved in an organic solvent. The materials are obtained from the Rohm & Haas Company, Philadelphia, the same company that supplies Rhoplex AC-33 to Bocour and Permanent Pigments, Inc. for their polymer tempera products, Aqua-Tec and Liquitex. Both the Magna and the polymer tempera media and colors are made from the same acrylic resin base. The essential difference is that Magna colors are oil-compatible, while polymer tempera is water-compatible.

Until recently it was not generally known that the binding ingredient in Magna paints is acrylic resin. Promotional material stressed the idea that Magna colors were "plastic" paints, but because of the unfortunate associations aroused by this term, the manufacturer decided to use the more esoteric but accurate term "acrylic resin" on the paint containers as well as in his advertising.

Leonard Bocour, the founder of the company that bears his name, is a unique authority on the subject of the materials of the painter. During the 1930's and early 1940's Mr. Bocour occupied a loft on 15th Street in New York City, just east of Fifth Avenue. He alternated between painting his own pictures and grinding or otherwise preparing oil colors for his friends and buyers who wanted a top grade, unadulterated painting medium. The American painter, Emil Ganso, had made Leonard Bocour aware of the importance of craft and had introduced him to Doerner's book in the original German edition.

Leonard Bocour's studio was always an interesting place to visit, filled as it was with the trappings of the craftsman's trade. Covering the walls in helter-skelter fashion hung an amazingly large collection of paintings by well-known contemporary American painters. Some of these painters helped to fill the paint tubes in their spare time. Once, while I was ordering some small item, Jack Levine, the contemporary painter, emerged from the shadows of Bocour's large studio-workshop. He cordially invited those present to visit his studio a few floors above, and while there, quickly dashed off a small drawing in illustration of a technical point he had made, which he allowed us to keep. On his easel was the now famous "Welcome Home." At that time Jack Levine was very enthusiastic about the "secret" formula of Tiepolo, as discovered by Jacques Maroger, the former technical director of the laboratory of the Louvre. Both Jack Levine and I had spent some time at the Baltimore Museum of Art, attempting to assimilate the lessons Professor Maroger was able to teach.

Leonard Bocour's studio-loft will always be remembered as a center of very serious and important work; this was not a commercial artists' supplies store dealing in "paint-by-the numbers" sets and animal drawing books. Today, Leonard Bocour is manufacturing a wide variety of quality products for the serious painter. These materials include oil paints, gesso, painting panels, watercolors, polymer tempera, and his important new painting medium, Magna colors. His is no longer a one-man operation.

In a recent interview arranged to discuss his acrylic resin paints, Leonard Bocour pointed out that since before the Italian Renaissance, little has changed in regard to pigments used in the manufacture of paints. Some colors, such as lapis lazuli, are too expensive for commercial use today, while others such as phthalocyanine blue, have recently begun to find favor. These instances are relatively rare. What has changed, however, and what will very likely continue to change, is the paint vehicle or binder. "I am constantly astounded," said Mr. Bocour, "at the attitudes of people living in the middle of the twentieth century. They refuse to believe that the centuries old oil medium may not be the last word in painting binders. Technological discoveries of this century have produced much new information and many new materials. It is foolish to believe that the artist will continue as he has in the past. These synthetics are *new* media; Magna differs from oil as casein differs from watercolor, or egg tempera differs from fresco. The new media have absolutely unique contributions to make."[1]

While it is true that Magna colors are distinctly different from all other media, the casual user will find it difficult to distinguish these acrylic resin paints from the traditional oil paints. The two are compatible; many painters use Magna paints for certain effects and oil colors for others, or they mix them together on the same painting. The acrylic resin medium is actually very similar chemically to what can be described as liquid Plexiglas or Lucite. When mixed with oil colors, each medium partakes of some of the qualities of the other.

Plexiglas is the trade-name of the clear, glass-like, acrylic resin product manufactured by Rohm & Haas. Lucite is an almost identical material marketed by the du Pont company. They are so similar that a trained inspector is unlikely to distinguish one from the other. Bocour Artist Colors, Inc., uses the Rohm & Haas product, but du Pont supplies a similar substance under the trade name of "Lucite 44." Art stores either have it in stock or can order this material. Unlike the Magna medium, Lucite 44 is sold in a dry state; the artist must dissolve the white, synthetic substance in toluene or xylene. This solution may then be diluted with linseed oil and turpentine. Most painters who use Lucite 44 mix this medium with tube oil colors, thereby gaining some of the advantages of the synthetic medium. Lucite 44 is used by some painters as a superior substitute for damar varnish. Although these uses of the Lucite 44 medium are valid enough, the wiser and more convenient

[1] Leonard Bocour, interview with the author, December 10, 1961.

course would seem to be to make use of the already formulated Magna colors and medium.

In order to provide a frame of reference for the further discussion of oil-compatible, acrylic resin paints, the following list of characteristics is provided:

1. They dry very rapidly.
2. They are compatible with linseed oil and turpentine.
3. They are soluble in turpentine long after they have dried, and may be softened and reworked at any time. Dried colors on the palette need not be wasted.
4. Impasto may be built up with no concern for permanency. Successive layers bind together chemically; new layers may be thick or thin as desired.
5. They will not yellow, crack, peel, or fade.
6. The working texture of these paints is very similar to oil paints, unlike the other new synthetic media.
7. They can be handled in imitation of the techniques of egg tempera, watercolor, gouache, fresco, and oil.
8. They may be used on a wide variety of supports.
9. They are more brilliant than oil colors. They may or may not change value when dry, depending upon the amount of binder used.

In order to provide an understanding of these oil-compatible, acrylic resin paints in relation to the traditional standard set by the oil medium, the above list should be measured in relation to this standard. The oil-compatible, acrylic resin medium has been found to provide a number of distinct advantages over the oil medium. The reader may decide for himself whether this new medium is as important as its proponents claim it to be.

1. Rapid drying is usually considered to be advantageous. Magna and Lucite 44 paints can be retarded only slightly by the addition of more medium. Only the addition of linseed oil or oil colors has much effect on drying time. This procedure, however, involves the risks inherent in the use of oil as a vehicle, a dis-

advantage that the use of the synthetics is supposed to eliminate. Unless the painter desires a rapidly drying medium, therefore, these new synthetics should not be used. But, if rapid drying is desirable, Magna and Lucite 44 are distinctly better than the traditional oil medium. Many painters are delighted by the rapidity with which a painting can be built up in these media. Weeks of work in the traditional oil medium can be accomplished in a single day of painting with synthetics. The teacher, too, will find that students are spared the technical difficulties inherent in the oil technique, enabling the young artist to devote all of his energies to the solution of esthetic problems. These acrylic resin paints will dry in less than two hours, more rapidly when thinned with turpentine. This characteristic is very useful in the classroom. Paintings may be stacked or carried soon after the paint is applied.

2. Many painters use Magna and Lucite 44 because they are compatible with oil colors; to these artists, this characteristic is a great advantage not available in the use of any other synthetic medium. The care with which an oil painting must be built up, however, limits the freedom associated with the use of these synthetic media alone. Even though they are compatible, the serious painter would be better advised to use the synthetic media without the oil adulterant.

3. The fact that the oil-compatible, acrylic resin paint film remains soluble in turpentine, even after long periods of drying time have elapsed, is an advantage as well as a disadvantage. Unlike oil paints, these colors need not be wasted if they develop a skin while standing on the palette. Turpentine will soften the skin, permitting the use of apparently hardened paint. If one wishes to soften an area in order to facilitate blending, turpentine will accomplish this end. Should these synthetic paints harden on the brush or clothing, turpentine will readily remove them.

The single disadvantage attending the ability of turpentine to dissolve these acrylic resin paints is the danger that someone may attempt to use turpentine as a cleaner, mistaking the synthetic painting for one in oil. The artist should label the back of an acrylic resin painting, warning that turpentine must *not* be used as a cleaner. Cleaning should be accomplished with the use of mild soap and water only.

4. Typical of the new synthetic media, in general, is the fact that the oil-compatible, acrylic resin paints can be built up with no thought to the relative thickness of the layers of paint. The following is a quotation from a Magna promotional piece, ". . . in Magna, the pigments are locked in the molecular structure of the vehicle. The color and the carrier are not simply blended; they are actually and ideally one!" Each successive layer bonds chemically with the underpainting, producing a homogeneous mass, free from the tensions that cause deterioration in the oil medium. When compared as to this specific property, the oil-compatible, acrylic resin paints are vastly superior to oil paints, and are equal to the "ideal medium" used as a theoretical standard in this book.

5. Some authorities dismiss the new synthetic media as "novelties," thereby overlooking the vast amount of work being done today in these media. The claims of the manufacturers that the oil-compatible acrylic resin paints will not yellow, crack, peel, or fade have not been disproved. On the contrary, all available evidence supports the belief that the acrylic resins are extremely durable. Mr. Bocour reports that his Magna colors have remained unchanged after a quartz-lamp Fadeometer test equal to 200 years of light exposure. Many serious painters have become convinced that the claims made for Magna are valid. Among those who have used Magna are Karl Zerbe, Mark Rothko, and Jackson Pollock in his late period. Although time will be needed to disprove all objections, the evidence indicates that at the very least, the acrylic resin paints will emerge as superior to oil from the standpoint of longevity. Chemists believe that they are able to determine the durability of the new synthetic media, while the weaknesses of linseed oil are also apparent to them. If the great hopes for these media prove true, the oil medium will almost certainly decline as a major painting vehicle.

6. Of all the synthetic media on the market today, the oil-compatible, acrylic resin paints are the only colors that possess a working consistency or texture almost identical with that of oil. For

(Courtesy of the Nordness Gallery. From The Johnson Collection.)

Fig. 8   "Dancing Commissar," by Karl Zerbe. A recent work by
the contemporary American painter, painted in Magna colors.

many painters, this is a strong recommendation. While some painters are stimulated by the fresh technical opportunities of the new
synthetic media, other artists whose interests are less tied to technique, find the familiar tactile qualities of the oil-compatible, acrylic
resin paints exactly to their order. The only differences in working
qualities of the oil and synthetic media begin to appear as the
acrylic paints rapidly set up. The effect is of telescoped time. If the
painter can work within these restrictions, these new paints offer no
problem. The ability of the artist to glaze, scumble, and thickly
overpaint with these acrylic colors within the span of a single day,
or even a few hours, is considered by many to be a great advantage,
especially when the effect is almost identical with oil.

7. Although it is usually considered bad practice to use one
medium in imitation of another, this dictum has not been applied to
the new synthetic paints. Long usage has clarified the potentialities
of the great traditional media, but this test of time has not been
applied to the new media. Because of the great versatility of the
new media, one cannot say at this time what methods of application
are peculiar to them alone. All that can be said now is that Magna
and Lucite 44 seem to be adaptable to a wide range of techniques
and effects.

If a moderate amount of medium is added to the Magna tube
colors, and if the painter works with the characteristic hatchings
and stipplings of the traditional egg tempera technique, the effect is
amazingly like egg tempera. To support this contention, one of my
own experiences is offered.

An egg tempera portrait had given me a considerable amount of
trouble due to the slow progress and thinness of the egg tempera
technique. In frustration, I decided to experiment with Magna. The
painting was very rapidly brought to a satisfactory finish indistinguishable from the surrounding egg tempera areas. This was a con-
vincing experiment; the subtlest difference would have been immediately apparent. Today, years later, there is still no change in
this two-medium painting. Not only is the effect of the differently
painted surfaces identical, but the Magna area has the appearance
of a well worked up passage, impossible to achieve in the egg tem-

pera medium unless a vast amount of time had been lavished upon it.

Very few painters have been able to sustain their interest long enough to enable them to produce a large egg tempera painting of superb technical quality. The egg tempera paintings which are most beautiful when considered from a technical point of view, are small. Andrew Wyeth, the leading contemporary exponent of the egg tempera medium, has painted one exceptionally large picture entitled "Soaring." It can be seen at the Webb Gallery of American Art, The Shelburne Museum, Shelburne, Vermont. Technically, the painting is thin and underpainted as compared with "The Trodden Weed," still owned by the artist. Since anything Wyeth paints can be sold for a very high price, it is reasonable to assume that "The Trodden Weed," a relatively small picture, has qualities that continue to inspire and instruct the artist.

If no medium is added to the tube paints, the effect of Magna colors is very similar to gouache or casein, especially if the paint is built up to the thicknesses usually associated with these media. If employed on a plaster wall, again without any medium added except that which is supplied by the manufacturer for proper tube consistency, the matte effect is remarkably like fresco. Unlike fresco, however, the acrylic resin mural is relatively unaffected by moisture, humidity, air pollution, and weathering.

Perhaps the most unexpected technique that can be imitated with Magna colors is transparent watercolor. The painter need only work on a typically rough watercolor support such as a good rag paper, dilute his tube colors with turpentine, and use no white pigment. All of the brilliance of the watercolor technique is available. Magna colors have qualities, however, that make this particular technique much more flexible than true watercolor. The turpentine will readily soften any previously applied wash, allowing the artist to blend other colors into it or, most useful of all, allowing the artist to rub the colors off the paper. This remarkable ability of the Magna colors to be removed with a simple wipe of a cloth saturated in turpentine eliminates the greatest handicap enforced by the traditional pure watercolor technique, namely, the difficulty or impossibility of correcting mistakes. Oil paint cannot be handled in this manner. Once the oil colors have set, turpentine will not act as a solvent. In addition, oil colors frequently deteriorate the paper.

If the artist chooses to use generous amounts of the Magna medium, the optical effect of the painted surface is indistinguishable from the appearance of oil paintings. Only chemical analysis could distinguish an oil passage from one painted in Magna colors. This amazing resemblance is also true of all the other techniques imitated by Magna; their resemblance to the traditional media is not merely approximate, they are virtually indistinguishable even when rendered side by side on the same painting. No other medium, traditional or synthetic, can equal this oil-compatible, acrylic resin paint in its wide versatility. Teachers, especially, should find this medium exceptionally useful.

8. Magna and Lucite 44 paints, like most other synthetic paints, are compatible with many different kinds of materials used as the support for painting. Canvas, illustration board, watercolor paper, Masonite, poured concrete, cement, plaster, brick, wood, and other related materials make good supports for these acrylic resin paints. Porous or roughened surfaces are best; smooth, glass-like materials are not recommended. Acrylic resin will appear at first to hold well on a slick surface, but defects will soon develop. Excellent grounds for sketching as well as for painting can be made by underpainting in Magna white or Magna gesso.

9. Magna and Lucite 44 paints are more brilliant and intense than colors ground in oil. Oil colors are mellow by comparison. This difference is apparently due to the yellowing effect of linseed oil; liquid acrylic resin is very clear. Leonard Bocour has said that some artists have complained that Magna colors are too bright, apparently not realizing that any color can be dulled, but that high chroma is difficult to achieve. A Magna painting does tend to become somewhat lighter in key, however, especially if little or no medium is added to the paints as they come from the tube.

Magna colors change value much in the same manner as do gouache and casein colors. The darker colors are much more affected by this phenomenon, drying considerably lighter. If work over a large, flat area is contemplated, the artist should mix enough color in the beginning. Color matching, if little medium has been used, is virtually impossible. Magna and Lucite 44 paints can equal oil in its ability to hold constant values upon drying if the artist will add sufficient medium. A final varnish also can help to hold the values constant.

Bocour Artist Colors, Inc., markets a remarkable varnish for use with these acrylic resin paints, or as a final varnish for oil paintings. Magna colors quickly develop a skin that is dry to the touch, but which can be picked up by roughly overpainting, especially if the new paint contains much turpentine or Magna medium. The Magna varnish has the remarkable property of immediately sealing off these fresh passages. Although it binds perfectly with the Magna medium, the varnish is as incompatible with the medium as oil is with water. The medium will not soften or dissolve the varnish. The varnish dries very rapidly and may be immediately overpainted. The varnish is also excellent for a final varnish if the desired effect is that of oil. If other effects are contemplated, such as gouache or water-color, the varnish is inappropriate.

The many advantages of these oil-compatible, acrylic resin paints make them ideal as instructional materials. They are fast-drying, versatile, bright, durable, and easily handled from the point of view of the classroom teacher. These paints deserve the popularity they have achieved.

7

Ethyl Silicate

The first artists to use synthetic media for serious work appear to be those from Mexico, especially David Alfaro Siqueiros, José Clemente Orozco, and José Gutiérrez. The first mural painted in a modern synthetic medium was the work of Siqueiros, completed in 1932 in Argentina. It was painted with a medium known as "silicate" which was applied according to the "Kaim" process, named after the discoverer. (This medium should not be confused with potassium or sodium silicate.)

In his limited edition of *From Fresco to Plastics,* José Gutiérrez tells of one of the incidents that prompted Siqueiros to experiment with a wide variety of synthetic media.[1] Returning unexpectedly from a journey, Siqueiros was surprised to find that some interested Americans had carried a number of his canvases outside and into the bright sunlight. Siqueiros was horrified to discover that his paintings in oil appeared very weak under the brilliant sun. He determined then and there never again to paint in a medium that could not stand up under these extreme conditions of light.

I have often noticed that my own work in the oil medium looks especially poor outdoors. Years ago, as a commercial artist, I would often be dismayed upon

[1] José Gutiérrez, *From Fresco to Plastics, New Materials for Easel and Mural Painting* (Ottawa: The National Gallery of Ottawa, Canada, 1956).

catching a glimpse of my paintings on the way to an interview with an art director. So sensitive to this factor was I, that I frequently postponed such a visit until the weather turned inclement. The dark, rainy weather not only made my work look better, but often aroused the sympathies of the art buyer! My recent experience with the new synthetics allows me to agree with Siqueiros; the new media *do* look well in very bright light.

Although it is possible to use ethyl silicate as a medium for easel painting, the Mexicans were especially interested in a medium that would stand up under extremes of weather. Gutiérrez and others had noted that automobile manufacturers, men who are vitally concerned with the weathering ability of paints, had long ago turned to the synthetic binders for their exterior finishes. Oil paint went out with the horse and buggy days. Leonard Brooks, José Gutiérrez and many other artists have painted pictures in both oil and a synthetic, allowing both to weather side by side. The reported results have always been the same. The synthetic painting changes little, if at all, during the period of time covered by the experiment. Other tests indicate that exterior exposure will ultimately weather even a synthetic painting, but much more time is required for this eventuality than in the experiments cited above.

José Gutiérrez was determined to investigate the potential of the silicates as painting media for outdoor murals. The Union Carbide Corporation provided him with pertinent information and supplied him with samples of their several products. Gutiérrez ultimately arrived at a formula of condensed ethyl silicate concentrate, hydrolized with alcohol, water, and hydrochloric acid. The technical details of this process are contained in the Gutiérrez book.

Ethyl silicate is a colorless, mildly odoriferous liquid. It is extremely resistant to heat and chemical fumes, and will not darken with age. When dry it develops an extremely tough surface; vigorous wire brushing will not remove an ethyl silicate film. The medium can be applied flat, modeled, scumbled, dry brushed, built up in heavy impastos, and textured in an infinite range of possibilities. Gutiérrez admits, however, that in formulating the medium great care and precision are required.

Fig. 9 "National Allegory," The National School for Teachers, Mexico, by José Clemente Orozco. A large exterior mural painted with ethyl silicate.

The ethyl silicate medium, as it was developed by Gutiérrez, was first used in Mexico in 1947 by the late José Clemente Orozco for a huge mural measuring more than 350 square meters. The mural serves as a background for an outdoor theater at the National School for Teachers. The wall on which the mural is painted faces north and acts as a windbreaker for a part of the building. Although the wall receives sunlight for about six hours daily, Gutiérrez reports that after nine years the colors remain unchanged.

For those who desire a more complete understanding of the medium, some technical instructions are offered. In order to proceed with the formulation of the painting medium, the artist must assemble these materials:

1. Condensed Ethyl Silicate (commercial grade). This fluid is sold in air-tight drums by the Union Carbon and Carbide Company. The color may at times appear cloudy, like tea with a drop of milk added, or it may be quite brownish in hue. After it has been mixed with alcohol, water, and acid, the medium becomes the color of Burgundy wine. The odor is then distinctly pleasant, and the color is very beautiful.
2. Denatured alcohol.
3. Water.
4. Hydrochloric acid. This is available in drug stores, hardware stores, and chemical supply houses. Plumbers use hydrochloric acid in the soldering process.

In addition to materials for the formulation of the medium, these utensils are necessary:

1. A graduated, cylindrical measuring glass.
2. A half-gallon glass jar.
3. A one-pint beaker.
4. A small tin or enamel funnel.

Slight mismeasurements can cause the medium to lose its binding power. Gutiérrez suggests that the artist keep a notebook with exact written data as the preparations progress. He also believes that test mixtures should be made in order to determine whether the materials used are of satisfactory quality. If the dried ethyl silicate film can withstand a vigorous scrubbing with a wire brush without powdering off, the medium is as it should be.

The formula for the ethyl silicate painting medium is given below. The quantities in parentheses will yield about 155 cc.:

1. 11 parts (110 cc.) ethyl silicate.

2. 3 parts (30 cc.) denatured alcohol (96% proof), or Synosol, available from the Union Carbon and Carbide Co.
3. 1 part (10 cc.) tap water.
4. ½ part (5 cc.) hydrochloric acid.[2]

These ingredients should be mixed in the order given. First pour the ethyl silicate and alcohol into a glass jar. Add the water and then the acid. Stir *once* only, with a clean stick or glass rod. In about five minutes the mixture will be heated to about 38° C. (100° F.). This will be cool enough to allow one to pick up the glass jar with unprotected hands. After 15 minutes have elapsed, test the mixture with the thumb and index finger. The medium should feel slightly sticky. If the medium does not heat or become sticky, something is wrong; either the proportions used are inaccurate or the alcohol is of poor quality. Synosol used in place of the alcohol will remove the danger of poor grade alcohol.

The medium can be used immediately, but it is better if permitted to stand for 12 hours. Enough medium should be made for a week's work, the amount depending upon the size of the mural or painting. Containers of the ethyl silicate medium should not be left open; gelatinization soon takes place if the air is permitted to circulate freely above the fluid. Very large amounts of the medium require somewhat less hydrochloric acid. Gelatinization should proceed very slowly if maximum adherence of the ethyl silicate is desired.

The following colors have been found to be exceptionally compatible with the ethyl silicate medium: Venetian red, Indian red, Puzzolian red, red iron oxides, all shades of yellow ochres, burnt or raw sienna, burnt or raw umber, all shades of cadmium yellow and red, cobalt blue, ultramarine blue and violet, cerulian, veridian, terre verte, chrome green, thalo green, vine and ivory black, and titanium dioxide white.

These colors should be obtained in dry pigment form and stored in glass jars. Immediately before working with these pigments, add one-fifth the volume of Celite #110 or Hyflo, both Johns Man-

[2] José Gutiérrez, *From Fresco to Plastics.*

ville products. Mixing is best accomplished by shaking until the powders are thoroughly assimilated by the pigment. These two additives remove excessive shine from the dried paint film and also add a very desirable body to the pigments. All the colors are intermixable; variety is limited only by the artist's ability.

Several surfaces are excellent as the support for a painting in ethyl silicate. All supports must be rigid. Poured concrete is perhaps the best, but cement walls, porous stone brick, and Masonite are also good. Cement walls must first be covered with a scratch coat formulated as follows:

1. 1 part gray or white cement (Portland type).
2. 2 parts rough marble dust or clean sand.
3. Add from 1/10 to 1/5 the volume of Celite #110 or Hyflo. Either will facilitate even setting and provide greater plasticity to the mixture.[3]

The final painting coat or ground should consist of the following, regardless of what material is used as the structural base:

Mix 1 part cement as above, 2 parts fine marble dust, and 1/5 part Celite #110 or Hyflo. This final coat may be made smooth, rough, or with a finish like emery cloth. This porous ground facilitates adherence of the paint film and therefore permanency.[4]

The wall must next be neutralized with hydrochloric acid in solution, one part acid to nine parts water. After 24 hours, wash the surface clean with water. When the wall is dry, draw the design with colored chalks or charcoal sticks. The pigment mixture can now be mixed with the ethyl silicate solution in a can or jar, or the dry colors can be dipped into with a brush moistened with the ethyl silicate medium and then mixed on a glass palette. The first method is best for large flat areas, the second method is most useful for details and modeling. Too much medium will produce an exces-

[3] José Gutiérrez, *From Fresco to Plastics.*
[4] *Ibid.*

sively glossy and weak paint film that will soon powder off. The artist can learn the correct proportions of pigment to medium only by experience.

No area should be overpainted until the undercoat is dry. The area should be scrubbed with a wire brush or rubbed with sandpaper in order to develop sufficient tooth for the best adhesion of the next coat. Corrections can be made by following the same procedure.

Color intensity should be kept stronger than one ultimately desires; like fresco, the colors lower in brightness after a little time. This is due to the fact that wet colors are deeper in hue than they are in the dry state.

Brushes should be cleaned after use with a detergent. Ethyl silicate will ruin a brush if allowed to dry on it. When not in use, brushes may be left in the pure ethyl silicate.

This medium can be used to great advantage on exterior walls of buildings, the bottoms or sides of swimming pools and fountains, or any other location where excessive moisture eliminates the use of other media. Traditional fresco would be impossible under any of these conditions. José Gutiérrez believes that once an artist learns to manipulate the ethyl silicate medium, he will never return to traditional fresco as a medium for mural painting.

The foregoing should make it clear that ethyl silicate is no medium for amateurs. The classroom teacher, whose needs require a direct, simple medium, would find ethyl silicate to be much too complicated a technique. The college teacher, however, may find that serious students are able to utilize the medium for exterior work that would be completely beyond the range of other media. Mexican students have created large murals in ethyl silicate; the many recent modern buildings in the United States could well have been enhanced if a few of their walls had been similarly decorated.

8

Pyroxylin

An increasingly important new synthetic medium is pyroxylin, known to the layman as "lacquer" and sold commercially under the trade-name of Duco. The Mexican painters have used this medium most successfully, beginning as early as the late 1920's. David Alfaro Siqueiros was the first well-known artist to use this new medium. His "Echo of a Scream," painted in 1937, and now owned by the Museum of Modern Art in New York City, is typical of the excellent paintings that have been created in pyroxylin. Jackson Pollock increased the stature of the medium by painting many of his large, tapestry-like canvases with the American product, Duco.

The early experimenters in the pyroxylin medium, or automobile lacquer as it was sometimes called, were not particularly successful. Siqueiros believes that some of his work cracked and darkened, as a result of the poor thinners then available. These automobile lacquers had been originally designed for commercial finishing processes which necessitate spraying techniques for their proper application. The spraying or laying in of flat areas of color is a very different process from that required by the artist's special needs, in which glazing, scumbling, underpainting, overpainting, heavy impasto, wiping out, etc., are vitally necessary. Some authorities held out very little hope for this particular synthetic medium, going so far as to say that no successful application of these materials to permanent artistic painting

98

Fig. 10 "Echo of a Scream," by David Alfaro Siqueiros. A fine example of a painting in Duco by the famous Mexican painter.

had so far been accomplished. This cautious attitude was perhaps well taken, but many of the pyroxylin paintings that are today in excellent condition were painted well before such doubts were published. During this same period many oil paintings have developed all of the defects to which the oil medium is heir.

Pyroxylin is not a new medium in the sense that polymer tempera and the other acrylic resin media are new. The medium was discovered over 100 years ago, although the commercial advantages of pyroxylin were not exploited in the wood and metal finishing industries until well into this century. The medium is produced in a number of ways, but the end product is about the same. A typical method is to treat cotton linters or high grade tissue paper with a mixture of concentrated sulphuric and nitric acids, partially diluted in water. Chemically, pyroxylin is the same as commercial gun cotton. The base is nitrocellulose.

The artist may purchase pyroxylin in most paint stores. The medium is sold on the basis of its viscosity, of which three common densities are useful to the painter. The heavy solution is the consistency of thick honey, the medium solution is rather syrupy, and the light solution has about the same viscosity as linseed oil. Their color is clear.

Supports for paintings executed in pyroxylin must be rigid; Celotex, Masonite, and wood panels of all kinds are excellent. Grounds should be made of a thinned solution of pyroxylin and may be sprayed or brushed on the support. Colored or toned grounds may be made by mixing the thinned pyroxylin solution with desired pigments. To thin, add one-twentieth to one-tenth the volume of Carbitol to the pure medium. In order to create a rough ground, mix the pigments and pyroxylin and add one-fifth the volume of Celite #110 or Hyflo. One should not use any but the best thinners available. A cheaper thinner may be purchased for the cleaning of brushes, etc.; these thinners are usually sold in three grades. Carbitol is an excellent thinner, solvent, and to some extent, a retarder. Castor oil, tetracresil of phosphate, Flexol D.O.P., and Lyndol may also be used as retarders. A teaspoonful to a quart of the pyroxylin medium is all that is needed.

According to José Gutiérrez, the best formula for a pyroxylin ground is the following:

Mix together two parts of medium viscosity pyroxylin, six parts thinner, and one part Carbitol. If additional retarder is necessary for smooth brushing, use a few drops of Flexol D.O.P. When applying this mixture, the artist must be sure to brush only once across the panel; repeated strokes will pick up the applied paint in a most unpleasant way. The ground dries to the touch in less than 15 minutes. If the artist decides to spray on the ground, a technique that is very useful in the preparation of mural base coats, the medium must be thinned to a consistency that will work well in the spray gun. In order to do this, mix one part heavy viscosity pyroxylin with one part light viscosity pyroxylin. Thin this mixture to the consistency of heavy milk. If the spray gun does not operate smoothly, add thinner until it does. This spray solution makes a very good sealer and ground for oil paintings as well as for paintings in pyroxylin.[1]

The medium for painting is formulated somewhat differently. Many variations are possible, but the following is a good basic formula: Mix either the heavy or the medium viscosity pyroxylin with an equal part of the light viscosity medium. Add another equal part of the best thinner available, and from 10 to 20 per cent of the total volume of Carbitol.

Pyroxylin works especially well with dry pigments; all those listed as useful in the chapter on ethyl silicate are compatible with this medium. If the artist prefers to reduce the excessively high gloss, he may mix two parts of the pigment selected with one part Celite #110 or Hyflo. Shake this mixture until the powders are well integrated. The powdered pigment and the Celite #110 or Hyflo will appear somewhat whitish, but once the medium has been added, the original color strength returns.

Celite #110 and Hyflo are ground, seashell substances used in industry as fillers. They are chemically inert and work very well with a variety of artist's media, including oil paints. They resemble

[1] José Gutiérrez, *From Fresco to Plastics.*

talc powder, and may be used up to one-fifth of the total mixture by volume. Celite #110 and Hyflo (produced by Johns Mansville) are known in the paint industry as "opaquers."

The technical range of the medium is surprising. Pyroxylin can be thinned down to the consistency of watercolor and actually used on watercolor paper. Unlike watercolor, however, unsuccessful passages may be wiped out with solvent and immediately repainted. Very heavy impasto may also be built up if the layers are kept reasonably thin. As much as one inch or more is possible. Marble dust, sawdust, threads and cotton, finely broken glass, glass beads, chopped Celotex, pebbles, paper, etc., may be incorporated into the paint film for their color and textural contributions. Celotex, wood, or Masonite can be roughed off with the teeth of a saw and the resultant dust can be sprinkled on the still wet surface. These particles will be well glued in the sticky paint and will form a most agreeable texture over which the artist can paint as soon as the pyroxylin undercoat dries.

Another excellent texture on which to paint can be made by pouring sand on a wet pyroxylin surface. The sand can even accomplish a certain amount of modeling if carefully poured through a tea strainer. Before the paint sets, tip the panel up and gently tap it against the floor or table top. The artist will do well to have previously covered the floor or table with newspapers in order to catch the loose sand. The loose and excessive sand will drop off evenly, leaving a beautiful, sandpaper-like ground. This method for making a sand ground is applicable to other synthetic media, especially polymer tempera.

Pyroxylin can also be used to imitate perfectly the effect of fine fresco. To achieve this result, the artist must first prepare a ground of white pyroxylin, as described earlier in this chapter. Next, using an airbrush or hand brush, apply a thin coat of the clear pyroxylin. To paint over this surface the artist need only dip the brush in clear thinner and mix the pigments to the colors desired. No medium is required, nor should it be used for the fresco effect. The binder is already on the wall. As the thinner and pigments are applied to the mural surface, the ground is dissolved sufficiently to bind the pigments. If the paint is applied with the appropriately light touch, the same quality as is found in fresco, the finest egg tempera, or casein can be achieved. Miguel Covarrubias, the Mexican painter, created two mural maps in the Hotel Del Prado, Mexico City, using this technique. The year was 1947; the murals have shown no deterioration.

The artist must be careful to use only reliable materials in these pyroxylin techniques if durable results are desired. Do not mix products sold under one trade-name with those of another company. Each producer employs different solvents and plasticizers as well as pigments. Some money can be saved if the artist mixes his own solvent, an important consideration in the case of a large mural. A good formula is the following:

Stir into solution two parts industrial alcohol, one part methyl alcohol, and one part benzol. This mixture should be stored in glass containers and kept under cover.

The preceding pyroxylin techniques are suitable only for those who are experienced painters. The casual practitioner would do well to avoid a medium of this kind with its manifold problems and delicately balanced formulas. For the average painter, and especially for the teacher who would like to make use of lacquer techniques, Duco automobile lacquers are recommended. The primary disadvantage is the limited color range available.

When ordering Duco, the artist must be sure to specify Duco automobile lacquer, and not the well-known Duco enamel. Buy the smallest cans obtainable in the beginning; later, those colors which have been found to work best can be bought in larger quantities. For those who may wish to seriously investigate the possibilities of the Duco medium, José Gutiérrez recommends the following color selection: white primer, heavy clear lacquer, medium clear lacquer, light clear lacquer, white clear lacquer (all the former should be bought in the quart size), and one-pint cans of black lacquer, ultramarine lacquer, Prussian blue lacquer, and maroon lacquer (the reddest variety obtainable). Since the writing of the Gutiérrez book, vermilion has become available. This red is especially useful to the artist who must work with a limited color range. There is no need to buy other than the basic colors listed here; all others in the Duco line are mixtures of the available primaries. Pigments may be added to the clear lacquers listed above in order to achieve a well-rounded palette.

The last decade has seen a marked improvement in the quality of the materials that are available to those interested in painting in pyroxylin. Results were reasonably good with the poorer materials; the painter today should be able to create works of excellent technical quality.

Pyroxylin's most outstanding characteristic, from the painter's point of view, is the medium's tremendously sensuous quality. There is nothing about the manner in which the artist can manipulate the medium that is at all familiar. The paint flows and sets up in peculiar ways. Some painters, finding that pyroxylin is in no way similar to oil, have prematurely discarded the medium without giving it a second chance. If Duco is used, the rapid drying can be controlled by the addition of du Pont Super Retarder. As understanding and skill are developed, most painters discontinue using any retarder, preferring the advantages of a rapidly drying paint.

Before beginning an ambitious work in pyroxylin, the artist or student would do well to conduct a series of tests on small Masonite panels. Masonite, like pyroxylin, has a cellulose base; many painters prefer to paint directly on this popular support material, "cellulose on cellulose." José Gutiérrez suggests that the experimenter spread a thin coat of white pyroxylin on the Masonite test panel and before it sets up, pour on another color. With a palette knife or inexpensive house painter's brush, manipulate this second layer over the undercoat. With an eye-dropper, scatter a few drops of the thinner over the surface. Study the unique technical effects obtained with these and any other manipulations that may come to mind. The artist may tilt, tap, or shake the panel; an infinite variety of swirls, drippings, blendings, and textures are available with these means. Add other colors and make note of their resemblance to smoke, sky and cloud effects, fire, and atmosphere. Knives, spoons, sticks, and rags can be helpful in producing other textures. While the paint is still tacky, the use of small squeegees, steel combs, flexible scrapers, and rollers can provide additional subtlety and variety.

An interesting ground can be made by spreading crumpled tissue or tracing paper over a wet coat of pyroxylin. The paper may be dipped in thinner and pressed against the dry prime coat for a similar effect. The result is a wonderfully wrinkled surface, ideal for a sensuously textured ground. Unwanted areas can be removed by pouring thinner onto the surface and, after a short period, scraping off the offending passage. The artist may press newspapers against the wet, thinner-loosened surface. When lifted off, most of the unwanted pyroxylin will be found adhered to the paper.

In the beginning, the painter will find that most of the effects obtained are more or less accidental. With practice, however, control develops and the artist then has at his command a truly amazing range of technical effects, most of which are very different from the technical clichés that have become so monotonous in the traditional media.

The artist will find that pyroxylin is adaptable to the needs of painterly techniques such as modeling, glazing, and scumbling. Colors may be mixed directly on the painting, or a porcelain palette may be used. The first attempts at painting in pyroxylin should be on horizontally supported panels. Later, when some proficiency has been developed, the artist may find a vertically supported surface helpful for certain techniques. If panels larger than nine square feet are used, the best practice is to brace them on the reverse side with strips of wood. If left unbraced, no matter what the size, panels should be stored flat in order to prevent warping.

For the painting of large murals, the Mexicans have found that a false wall is frequently a more convenient support than the wall itself. Masonite is fastened to wooden strips which are then attached firmly to the wall. The seams between the panels must be covered with strips of cloth which are glued into place with pyroxylin. The Mexican muralists have painted many impressive works in this manner.

Because the highly inflammable fumes accompanying the use of pyroxylin are very likely to give one a headache, work in this medium should be pursued in a very well-ventilated area. This unfortunate characteristic of the medium must be taken into consideration when pyroxylin is to be used as an instructional material. No flame must be allowed near the liquids used in pyroxylin painting. Cold cream should be rubbed into the hands if any extensive work in the medium is contemplated; the lacquer will then be easily removed from the skin with a cloth soaked in thinner. Wash all areas exposed to the medium with soap and water.

Should the paint harden in the can, the solvent will restore the original consistency in a few hours. The semi-hardened paint can be useful in the building up of heavily textured passages.

Although pyroxylin is used in the automotive industry for exterior finishes, the medium is not recommended for exterior murals. Automobile paints are generally considered to have a life expectancy of about 10 to 12 years, or the life of the average car. The interior life expectancy of Duco should be excellent, however. No serious defects have appeared in important works painted in this medium.

Some authorities report that cellulose nitrate is not stable in bright light, especially strong sunlight. The paint film becomes excessively acid in time, brittleness increases, tensile strength decreases, and the film yellows. Cellulose nitrate, especially in the form of celluloid lacquer, has been used as an adhesive and impregnating agent in the restoration of museum objects for over 50 years. These uses, however, have not involved light exposure.

To sum up: Pyroxylin is a dynamic new medium that has hardly been investigated from the standpoint of its esthetic range and technical possibilities; the medium offers many opportunities for the young artist searching for a personal idiom.

9

Vinyl Acetate

Vinyl acetate, a paint binder sold under the trade-name of Vinylite, has been used successfully by many artists for mural and easel painting. Vinyl acetate is not a medium for the casual painter; exact formulas and precise techniques must be employed if worthwhile work is to result. The materials necessary for the formulation of the medium are products of the Union Carbide Chemical Corporation. This synthetic resin is particularly stable to the effects of both heat and light and is resistant to weak acid, alkaline, and salt solutions. From the point of view of the muralist, the outstanding property of the vinyl acetate medium is its ability to adhere to a wide variety of surfaces. The largest mural in Canada was recently painted in vinyl acetate by York Wilson.

Vinyl acetate is supplied in a number of grades depending upon the molecular weight and degree of polymerization. It is a thermoplastic resin; softening temperatures, solution viscosity, and toughness increase with ascending molecular weight. The medium is free from acidity, and stable in storage, an important commercial factor. Because of these many desirable qualities, vinyl acetate resins are used as the base for nontarnishing metallic inks and lacquers.

There are two very similar forms of the vinyl acetate medium that are suitable for fine painting. These are designated by the manufacturer with the initials A.Y.A.F. and A.Y.A.T. A.Y.A.T. is merely a heavier material on the molecular scale. Their appearance is quite similar; A.Y.A.F. resembles rock salt, while A.Y.A.T. has more the appearance of hailstones. The same materials can be bought in liquid form. When sold under the trade-name of Vinylite, the vinyl acetate solution has the consistency and color of a perfectly clear, honey-like substance. A similar product is sold under the trade-name of Vinylseal. There are no chemical differences between the liquid forms of vinyl acetate and the dissolved A.Y.A.F. and A.Y.A.T. form. From the point of view of cost, however, the artist will find that the dry forms of vinyl acetate are more economical.

The dry forms of vinyl acetate must be dissolved in and placti-cized with the following solvents: industrial acetone, denatured alcohol, butanol or butylic alcohol, Carbitol and Synasol.

The artist must also have these articles at hand before beginning the dissolving process; a small scale, a measuring glass, several stirrers (glass rods or clean wood), a gallon-size tin can, two one-gallon containers with lids, and an electric hot plate.

The following procedure and amounts of ingredients will enable the artist to make two quarts of the painting medium at a cost of about two dollars a quart:

First measure out 100 g. of A.Y.A.F. or A.Y.A.T. crystals on the small scale. The dissolving process will be greatly facilitated if the crystals are soaked overnight in a little alcohol. Next, add 200 cc. of the industrial acetone to the A.Y.A.T. or A.Y.A.F. crystals in the one-gallon tin can. Because industrial acetone is a very powerful solvent, the artist must be careful not to use more than 250 cc. of this solvent to each 100 g. of A.Y.A.T. or A.Y.A.F. crystals. Without boiling, heat the can and its contents on the hot plate, stirring constantly until the crystals are completely dissolved. The dissolving process can be accomplished without the hot plate, but a great deal more time is required.

Next, add 250 cc. to 500 cc. of denatured alcohol or Synosol. According to the viscosity desired, more or less of these liquids may be added. Be careful, however, not to exceed the upper limit of 500 cc. for each 100 g. of crystals used. To this mixture add 20 cc.

of butanol and 20 cc. of Carbitol for each 100 g. of the original measurement of the dry crystals. The medium is now ready for painting. Should the artist find that the consistency described in this formula dries too rapidly for his particular way of working, a few drops of Carbitol may be added to this mixture as the work progresses.

There are two basic methods for working in vinyl acetate, depending upon the size of the finished painting. If the area to be covered is large, the artist should mix the medium with the various pigments to be employed, and store them in small jars or cans. A complete range of the necessary colors can thus be prepared at the same time. The artist may use any of the pigments listed as useful for painting in ethyl silicate on page 95. Many other pigments are probably compatible with the vinyl acetate medium, but they have not been as thoroughly tested as have the listed pigments.

If smaller quantities of color are required, the artist should set up a palette of dry pigments in small cups. This kind of palette is available in most art stores; the depressions are stamped into a sheet of metal or molded in plastic.

Large areas can be brushed on flat as one would handle poster paint. When the medium is used for painting easel-size works, the best technique most closely resembles that of egg or casein tempera.

If one has never worked in this medium, several experiments are advised:

Cut up a series of small cardboard panels (6″ x 10″). Pour a small quantity of the vinyl acetate medium into a glass, and into another glass pour a little denatured alcohol. Bristle brushes are advised; they will withstand the powerful action of the chemicals better than the softer sable or camel's hair brushes. Cleaning is easily accomplished in alcohol.

Next, moisten the brush in the vinyl acetate medium. Dip the brush into the desired color and apply to the cardboard panel. Observe how the paint flows and reacts as it is manipulated. At first the medium will seem to dry too fast, but as competence is attained, the rapid drying will become an advantage. When the first coat has dried, brush a second layer over the panel using a different color. Two or more colors may be mixed together on an enamel or glass palette. Experiment with dry brush, scumbling, and glazing effects. The artist will observe that the brush strokes do not change their forms while drying as is the case in many of the traditional media; the brush strokes remain exactly as applied. Vinyl acetate is very different from oil and should not be handled with traditional attitudes in mind.

The vinyl acetate paint film remains remarkably flexible. If the medium is used on paper, the painting can be rolled into a tight scroll no matter how thickly the artist may have piled the impasto. The paint film will not crack or wrinkle. Almost any nongreasy or nonoily surface is suitable as a painting support for vinyl acetate. Some excellent materials are watercolor paper, tissue paper, cellophane, textiles such as cotton, silk, and wool (not rayon, a synthetic; the medium will attack and dissolve the fibers), frosted glass, unglazed terra cotta, parchment, unprepared canvas, plaster of Paris surfaces and walls, wood, brick, and stone. Most of these grounds do not need any special sealer or other preparation. Vinyl acetate it its own best sealer. If a colored ground is desired, the pigments and medium may be applied as a flat coat over the unprepared support.

A great variety of textural effects can be achieved in much the same manner as described in the chapter on pyroxylin. The palette knife is very useful, as are the many other utensils described on the same pages. The colors may be applied layer upon layer indefinitely without compromising permanency. The thinnest, most transparent glazes are also easily accomplished.

Should the artist wish to isolate the ground because of excessive absorbency, pyroxylin primer is useful, or add 10 to 20 per cent of the ethyl silicate medium to the vinyl acetate medium. José Gutiérrez, a pioneer in this medium, reports this latter mixture has been tested in the laboratory for periods and conditions equal to 7000 hours of continuous rain and ultraviolet radiation.[1] The paint

[1] José Gutiérrez, *From Fresco to Plastics.*

had been applied over sheet rock, a building material. *No* deterioration resulted from this severe test.

Vinyl acetate mixed with titanium white provides an excellent ground coat for oil or tempera paintings. This mixture may be easily applied over unprimed Masonite, Celotex, or unprepared canvas. The flexibility inherent in the vinyl acetate medium is especially useful when one is working on canvas.

If a fine, even gloss is desired, a heated iron worked over the surface of the finished vinyl acetate painting will produce this result, especially if the painting has been executed on paper or cloth. The vinyl acetate medium is an excellent primer for any surface on which oil is to be used. The medium also makes an excellent varnish for watercolors, casein, and tempera paintings as well as for vinyl acetate works.

Varnish coats should be applied with a soft brush or atomizer. Care must be taken that the medium does not soften and lift off some of the paint. The artist must be careful to brush on the varnish with parallel strokes; a small area should be experimented with before attempting a more ambitious application. The vinyl acetate medium may also be poured onto a horizontally supported painting surface and spread out with a smooth-edged piece of cardboard. If one coat of varnish does not produce the desired gloss, the second coat may be applied in from one to two days or when the first coat is firmly dry. A matte surface is obtainable by means of the addition of Celite #110 or Hyflo to the pigments before they are mixed with the vinyl acetate medium. Celite #110 and Hyflo will also add a most desirable body and weight to the pigments.

Vinyl acetate is not altogether new in the field of the fine arts. The medium has been used extensively by museums for the restoration of valuable paintings, and for the sealing of supports used to stiffen wood panels and canvas stretchers. If vinyl acetate is to be used as an adhesive, the butanol and alcohol should be eliminated when the medium is formulated. Another interesting use of vinyl acetate is in the preparation of colors to be applied to textiles. Pigments so applied will not wash out if the washing is done with reasonable care, although their brilliance may be softened a little. Classes in textile design should be able to make good use of this medium.

Although murals painted outdoors in the vinyl acetate medium will last for some time, such use is not recommended. If a similar medium is desired that will permit exterior painting, vinyl chloride acetate is indicated. This medium is discussed in the next chapter.

If the support for a mural in the vinyl acetate medium is to be plaster of Paris, the plaster surface should be neutralized by means of an application of acetic acid or ordinary cooking vinegar. An approved mixture is 10 to 20 per cent acetic acid or vinegar diluted in water. When the plaster surface is completely dry, the artist should seal the support with clear vinyl acetate. The vinyl chloride V.Y.H.H. medium, discussed in the next chapter, is also recommended for the sealing of walls when used either clear or pigmented.

When the prime coat has dried, the design may be drawn on the wall with charcoal or colored chalks. Because a mural is much more appropriate as an adjunct to architecture if the painting has no surface shine, the muralist will do well to mix in Celite #110 or Hyflo with the pigments before adding the medium. Not only will the finished surface be more attractive, but the pigments will work better because of a more desirable body.

Another good wall surface can be made with Masonite. This material has the advantage of being portable should the mural be desired somewhere else. Masonite allows the artist to paint in his studio, although many muralists insist that the best work can be done only in the actual architectural setting where the same light conditions by which the mural will ultimately be seen prevail. Masonite or Celotex (a less dense wall board) may be attached to the wall by means of wooden strips. These materials may be painted upon directly, since vinyl acetate is its own sealer, or an interesting surface can be made by gluing thin, unbleached muslin or canvas to the surface. A recommended glue is one of the synthetic, water dilutable varieties. The polymer tempera medium would be appropriate for this gluing job.

If vinyl acetate is to be applied to cement or concrete, a material used increasingly in the construction of modern buildings, the wall should be neutralized with hydrochloric acid. A recommended strength is 10 to 20 per cent diluted in water. After a thorough application of this solution, the surface should be permitted to dry before it is rinsed with a final dousing of clear water. When it is again dry, the artist should apply a sealing coat of vinyl chloride acetate, V.Y.H.H. The clear solution may be used or the addition of pigments may provide a toned ground.

There are almost no manipulative limits imposed by the vinyl acetate medium. The medium is much less expensive than are oil paints, a factor that can be of significance in the making of large murals.

Although vinyl acetate is less difficult to formulate than is ethyl silicate, the medium is too complicated technically to allow fruitful use by students under college age. The teacher is better advised to employ media such as pyroxylin or polymer tempera, materials that are easily obtained and easily manipulated.

10

Vinyl Chloride Acetate

Vinyl chloride acetate is another medium available to the painter which is sold under the trade-name of Vinylite and manufactured by the Chemicals Division of the Union Carbide Corporation. Unlike vinyl acetate, vinyl chloride acetate is recommended for outdoor and semi-outdoor mural painting. The medium is not only advised for areas where other paints would not survive because of rigorous atmospheric conditions, but it is also very satisfactory as an easel painting medium. One might ask why it is not advisable to use vinyl chloride acetate for all purposes rather than bother with vinyl acetate. José Gutiérrez answers this question by saying that he does not believe in using a medium whose properties are far beyond the needs of the particular job. Vinyl acetate will do very well for indoor painting; reserve the tougher medium for undertakings that require tougher qualities in the paint film.

Vinyl chloride acetate resins possess extra chemical inertness. They are unaffected by alkalis, oxidizing agents, most inorganic acids, water, alcohol, grease, and fats. Vinyl chloride acetate can be dissolved by the ketones, chlorinated hydrocarbons, and certain organic acids. When employed as a binder for paints, vinyl chloride acetate produces a tough, glossy, chemically resistant finish. The medium has the unique ability to adhere to metal, cloth, paper, and concrete as well as to all of the support materials recommended for vinyl acetate.

114

As was the case with the previously discussed vinyl acetates, vinyl chloride acetate is available in two types: V.M.C.H. and V.Y.H.H. These two media are very similar physically and chemically. V.M.C.H. can be used alone or in combination with V.Y.H.H. The V.M.C.H. vehicle is better suited to the requirements of a prime coat than is the other; as such, the medium may be mixed with pigment for a toned ground if desired. Both media have the appearance of granulated sugar, but their granules are much harder. The artist may easily confuse one with the other; labeling will prove especially helpful in this case.

Other variations on these vinyl resins are recommended for serious painting by the manufacturer, the Union Carbide Corporation. Although there is no reliable evidence that these media have been successfully experimented with in techniques useful to the painter, there is no reason to doubt that these additional media may prove to be as excellent as the others. Not only are new media constantly appearing on the market, but new pigments and analine dyes, with a far greater range than can be achieved with traditional coloring agents, are also entering the market in great numbers. Few have been adequately tested for permanency and handling ease by professional artists, but there is little doubt that they soon will augment the artist's media and perhaps drastically change his traditional attitudes toward color.

Both the V.M.C.H. and V.Y.H.H. compounds are dissolvable in the same solvents. One of the best solutions for this purpose is methyl isobutyl ketone. As was the case with the previously discussed vinyl acetate resins, the solvent for vinyl chloride acetate is the regulator of viscosity.

The painting medium is prepared as follows:

Use 100 g. of either of the two resins, and from 250 cc. to 500 cc. of methyl isobutyl ketone. Add the granular powder to ½ of the solvent to be used, and stir. Add the remaining solvent from time to time as the stirring process is continued. Stir constantly to avoid lumpiness. A mechanical mixer can be very helpful at this stage. Gutiérrez suggests a propeller attachment affixed to the bit of a hand electric drill. Such an instrument can be moved about for thorough mixing, unlike the usual motor-driven beater.

No other ingredients or plasticizers are necessary. The medium, prepared as directed here, should make a very good vehicle for brush application. The medium is a clear, colorless liquid. If the medium proves difficult to handle for a variety of reasons, as much as 1000 cc. of methyl isobutyl ketone may be added for each 100 g. of the V.M.C.H. or V.Y.H.H. resin used. As with so many of the synthetics, the artist will find that Celite #110 or Hyflo mixed with the dry pigments greatly improves the texture of the vinyl chloride acetate paint film. Special care must be taken to see that the powders are mixed together evenly and thoroughly, otherwise an uneven surface gloss will result.

Easel paintings should be painted as suggested in the chapter on vinyl acetate. The brush is wet in the medium, dipped into the pigments, mixed together on a palette, and applied to the support. Surface effects are similar to those achieved with the vinyl acetate medium.

Large pictures or murals should be painted with colors that have been mixed at the beginning of each day's work. To prepare the colors for this kind of use, pour an appropriate quantity of the medium into a can and add enough pigment for the desired consistency. No specific proportions are necessary because the pigments vary in their ability to absorb the medium. The dry paint film may be tested for adequate medium content by rubbing the hand over the surface. If any of the pigment powders off, more medium should have been used. Due to the excellent binding ability of the vinyl chloride acetate medium, however, powdering off is rare. The pigments used should be the same as those recommended for use with the vinyl acetate medium. Many others would probably work well too, but there are no reliable records of test results.

José Gutiérrez, a pioneer in this medium, reports that an exterior mural was painted in Mexico in 1948 with the vinyl chloride acetate medium. The work was begun on cement that was only 12 hours old. The wall faces the south and receives an average of seven hours of sunlight daily. All the colors used have successfully weathered eight years of exposure, with the lone exception of chrome green which has darkened.[1]

The remarkable ability of the vinyl chloride acetate medium to withstand outdoor conditions makes its use in mural painting very desirable. No data are available as to how long the medium will survive outdoors, but indications are that it surpasses all other media with the exception of ceramic tile.

The best supports for vinyl chloride acetate paintings are concrete, brick, and porous stone. If a special finish is required, especially on a brick wall, the artist will find that a scratch coat is necessary. A simple mixture for this purpose can be made and applied by a competent mason.

Mix three parts rough marble dust with one part cement and fiber, and add one-fifth the total volume of Celite #110. When applied properly, this mixture provides a hard, rough surface. This rough coat should be allowed to dry thoroughly before adding a final coat or ground over it.

The final coat is mixed as follows: Two parts fine marble dust are mixed into one part cement and one-fifth to one-tenth the total volume of Celite #110. This final coat can be worked to a sandpaper-like finish, or it may be troweled out smoothly. Most painters enjoy the textural effects obtainable on the rougher surface, but for some effects the smoothest possible surface may be preferred. After this final coat has dried, the ground should be neutralized with a 20 per cent hydrochloric acid solution diluted in water. Rinse thoroughly when dry.

The final ground coat is ideal for drawing and painting. Charcoal and colored chalks are good media for the laying in of the design. If the wall is too porous, the artist will find that a brushed or sprayer coat of clear V.M.C.H. over the surface is helpful. The more V.M.C.H. used in this application, the better; successive paint layers will adhere more satisfactorily to a rich underlayer of medium. For mural painting on the surfaces described here, the V.M.C.H. medium should be used for the base coats, and the V.Y.H.H. medium applied with the pigments for the final painting

[1] José Gutiérrez, *From Fresco to Plastics.*

layers. Some painters may prefer to mix one-half of the V.M.C.H. liquid with one half of the V.Y.H.H. liquid. Individual manipulative preferences should guide the painter in his own formulations.

The only precaution necessary is this: The brush must be used lightly or it will pick up the undercoat. The medium is a very powerful solvent for the dry underpainting. Marble dust, cement, pieces of glass, or any other inert material listed in other chapters may be mixed with the medium for added textural effects.

The low cost of materials required for this technique make it especially desirable for the painting of large murals. Other uses have also been found for the artistic use of vinyl chloride acetate resins. In 1950, Gateria Ortiz Monasterio, a Mexican sculptor, exhibited a number of terra-cotta pieces that had been polychromed with Vinylite. The results, as reported by José Gutiérrez, were excellent. They were shown at the Galeria de Arts, Mexico City, and received enthusiastic critical acclaim.[2]

The medium has also been satisfactorily used as a varnish for traditional fresco paintings; fresco murals appear to revive and brighten when so treated.

Of the three media, ethyl silicate, vinyl acetate, and vinyl chloride acetate, the last is by far the easiest to formulate. Therefore, if the teacher or student desires a medium in this category, vinyl chloride acetate is decidedly the most convenient. Its exceptional toughness lends the medium to uses beyond the range of the other two media. Because of these qualities, there is every likelihood that the vinyl chloride acetate resins will become increasingly popular as fine art media. At present, however, few painters are aware of their existence.

2 José Gutiérrez, *From Fresco to Plastics.*

11

Fiberglas Supports

"Painting is a two-dimensional art, but exhibitions give us more and more works classified as 'painting' that are actually three-dimensional," wrote John Canaday in his *New York Times* column.[1] Contemporary painters have increasingly turned from traditional supports to synthetic materials such as Masonite. But not until very recently have the polyester and epoxy resins been employed in the creation of supports with markedly sculptural characteristics. The contemporary American painter, James Kearns, has created a number of works in relief with these molding and laminating plastics. The trade-name of the best-known material in this field is Fiberglas, a product of the Owens-Corning Fiberglas Corporation.

Fiberglas is produced in a variety of forms, including sheets, rolls of matted glass fiber, loose chopped fibers, and the well-known woven cloth, which is available in a variety of weights. The matted glass fiber and the loose chopped fibers are used for building up thickness and the filling in of small hollows and depressions.

Fiberglas is made of fine thread-like fibers which have been drawn from molten glass. These fibers have enormous tensile strength, but are weak under a compression load. When woven into a cloth, Fiberglas is able to withstand a high degree of tension. Although polyester and epoxy have very poor tensile strength,

[1] *New York Times,* January 7, 1962. Reprinted by permission.

119

they have a high resistance to compression. When the glass cloth and the resin are combined, an extraordinarily tough material results, combining great impact, flexural, and tensile strengths.

The structural system of Fiberglas is analogous to that of reinforced concrete. Concrete alone is a very poor material when placed under tension; however, steel rods imbedded in it provide this strength. The great resistance of concrete to compression provides the complementary strength. Fiberglas and the resins, like reinforced concrete, ideally combine materials which provide high resistance to compression and tension.

The polyester and epoxy resins have slightly different characteristics. The epoxies are used if contact with metal is desired because they cling tightly to metals, a quality not held by the less expensive polyesters.

Most plastics require heat in order to create a "set." The resins used in the Fiberglas process do not. Both the polyester and the epoxy resins are applied wet, then permitted to dry for a firm bond.

The procedure for building a Fiberglas painting support is as follows:

The artist begins by building a mold with the three-dimensional features desired. The mold can be made of papier-mâché, wood, screening, metal rods, or any other materials which can be assembled to create the desired effect. Some artists may find preliminary studies useful before beginning the final construction; others may prefer to improvise as the work develops. No convolutions or indentations should be used which will not allow the easy separation of the finished Fiberglas support from the mold. An exception to this rule, however, permits tearing or cutting the mold away, section by section.

When the mold is completed, it should be sealed with any one of a variety of materials which will close the pores and prevent absorbency. Clear lacquer is recommended. When the sealer has dried, a coat of floor wax can be applied to the mold in order to permit easy removal of the finished Fiberglas form. Parting or releasing agents are available under a number of different tradenames if wax is not available.

With conventional Fiberglas constructions, such as boat hulls or chairs, the builder must pay close attention to the surface of the mold in order to assure a smooth finish for his product. A smooth surface for the painting support is not necessary, however, unless the artist so desires. In painting, since texture is usually desirable, the painter will probably want to use the rough side of the finished Fiberglas support, which is built up *away* from the mold. An endless variety of textural effects can, thereby, be worked into the support as the form develops.

An artist may easily obtain the resins and the Fiberglas cloth needed for building the support. Plastics houses and marine supply stores are among those suppliers providing the necessary materials and instructions.

After obtaining the Fiberglas cloth of the desired weight (heavy for a large, light for a small support), the artist cuts the cloth into shapes which his experimentation indicated will fit the mold. Strips are often the best because they can be criss-crossed and made to conform to a wide range of convolutions. Compound-curved surfaces, for instance, cannot be made wrinkle-free with a single, uncut piece of Fiberglas cloth.

Only after all the above preparations have been made should the resin be mixed with the required catalyst and accelerator. Once these materials have been mixed as directed, only 15 to 30 minutes remain before the resin becomes unmanageable. Therefore, the artist must be ready to apply the resin at once. The following is typical of the various methods required for mixing the resin:

First, add the catalyst to the resin. The mixing should be slow in order to prevent the development of undesirable air bubbles. The artist next adds the accelerator in the same careful manner. Instructions will usually emphasize that the catalyst and the accelerator must not be mixed together first. Some of these materials are highly explosive when so combined.

Two methods are useful in applying the resin to the Fiberglas cloth. The cloth may be dipped, in which case a suitable flat pan is needed to hold the resin. A more common procedure is to brush a coat of resin onto the surface of the mold and then to lay the glass cloth against the wet surface. Next, the artist applies one or two coats of resin over the cloth. It is important that the glass fibers be thoroughly impregnated with the resin; insufficiently coated areas will remain white, requiring additional brushings. A very smooth surface can be made by pressing Saran Wrap or cellophane against the wet resin and smoothing it out with the hand or a flat, clay modeling tool. Some individuals with sensitive skin find that they must protect their hands with rubber gloves, especially if the resin is an epoxy.

If the support is removed from the mold after only one layer of Fiberglas and resin has been applied, an additional application of the cloth and resin may be necessary in order to achieve sufficient rigidity. Experience will indicate the extent to which the support must be strengthened. It is not necessary to wait for the underlayer to dry completely before applying the next coat; however, the first layer must be thoroughly dry before the mold can be removed. The resins will set up at room temperature; heat lamps or the sun will accelerate the process. The Fiberglas support is sufficiently dry when the surface cannot be dented with the fingernail.

The artist may wish to further texture the support before beginning to paint. The loose fibers or finely cut pieces of the Fiberglas cloth and the resin can be mixed into a paste, then kneaded, troweled, scraped, or modeled into textural effects of great variety, much as one would work with clay. These rough surfaces are ideal for the adhesion of the subsequent paint layers.

A wide variety of pigments and binders are chemically consistent with a Fiberglas support. Because the support is chemically inert, one need only be sure that the surface is not too slick for proper paint adhesion. A sandpapered surface is often desirable. Thin films of color may be rubbed into the surface of the Fiberglas support with the fingers, or the paint may be heaped on. Although oil paints could be used, one of the synthetic binders is probably more appropriate. The acrylic resin paints, in any of their forms, are excellent for this purpose.

As these new materials are mastered by contemporary artists there seems little doubt that a great variety of support surfaces will eventually become commonplace. Painters are no longer limited to two-dimensional spaces on which to develop their ideas.

"A new art means only new forms, and new forms arise from one or both of two causes: new needs and new possibilities."[2] The esthetic standards of our time allow directions which, until very recently, would have been thought highly undesirable, even if technically possible. Support construction, as well as the new synthetic paints, are almost certain to alter profoundly the traditional appearance of paintings before this century has run its course.

---

[2] Jacques Barzun, "Modern Architecture: The Road to Abstraction," *Columbia University Forum*, IV, 14.

Appendix

A. Sources of Materials

The following list of materials includes only those that are less familiar, or that might not be available in the average art store. If an item is not available locally, the manufacturer will usually supply it directly (and often at considerable savings), or suggest a regional dealer.

Material	Source
1. accelerator (Fiberglas)	Plastics supply house or boating supplies.
2. acetic acid	Chemical supply house.
3. acetone	Chemical supply house.
4. alcohol (butylic, denatured, industrial, or metyl)	Chemical supply house.
5. Aqua-Tec (Bocour Artist Colors, Inc.)	Art supply store.
6. asbestos	Building supplies.
7. benzol	Chemical supply house.
8. butanol	Chemical supply house.
9. Carbitol (Union Carbide Chemical Corp.)	Chemical supply house.
10. catalyst (Fiberglas)	Plastics supply house or boating supplies.

11. Celite (#110 or #289) (Johns Manville, Inc.) — Building supplies or commercial paint stores.

12. Cellosize (WSLM grade) — Borden Company, Chemical Div., Foster St., Peabody, Mass.

13. Celotex (commercial wallboard) — Building supplies.

14. Color Aid — Art supply stores.

15. Color Vue — Art supply stores.

16. condensed ethyl silicate (commercial grade) — Chemical supply house.

17. Duco (lacquer) — Automobile paint supply stores.

18. du Pont Super Retarder — Commercial paint store or chemical supply house.

19. epoxy resin — See "Fiberglas."

20. ethyl silicate — See "Vinylite."

21. expanded mica — Building supplies.

22. Fiberglas (Owens-Corning Fiberglas Corp.) — Plastics houses or boating supply houses.

23. Flexol D.O.P. — Chemical supply house.

24. hydrochloric acid — Chemical supply house.

25. Hyflo (Johns Manville, Inc.) — Building supplies or commercial paint stores.

26. Kaolin (clay) — Pottery supply store.

27. Lestoil — Household supplies.

28. Liquitex (Permanent Pigments, Inc.) — Art supply store.

29. Lucite (du Pont) — Art supply store.

30. Lyndol — Chemical supply house.

31. Magna colors (Bocour Artist Colors, Inc.) — Art supply store.

32. Masonite (commercial wallboard) — Building supplies.

33. methyl isobutyl ketone — Chemical supply house.

34. Museum Quick-On Gesso	Art supply store.
35. Naconal R.S.F. (wetting agent)	National Aniline, Inc., Somerville, Mass.
36. parting agents (Fiberglas)	Plastics supply house or boating supplies.
37. Perlite (expanded mica)	Building supplies.
38. plaster of Paris	Building supplies.
39. Plexiglas (Rohm & Haas, Inc.)	Plastics supply house.
40. Politec (José Gutiérrez, Calle Tigre No. 24, Mexico 12, D.F.)	The Politec Co., 2255 Polk St., San Francisco, California.
41. Polyco 953–7 A	Borden Company, Chemical Div., Foster St., Peabody, Mass.
42. polyester resin	See "Fiberglas."
43. Portland cement	Building supplies.
44. releasing agents (Fiberglas)	Plastics supply house or boating supplies.
45. Resoflex 296	Cambridge Industries, Cambridge, Mass.
46. Rhoplex AC-33	Rohm & Haas Company, Phila., Penn. (Minimum order: 55 gallons.)*
47. Saran Wrap (Dow Chemical Co.)	Household supplies.
48. Styrofoam (Dow Chemical Co.)	Plastics supply house.
49. Synosol	Chemical supply house.
50. tetracresil of phosphate	Chemical supply house.
51. toluene	Chemical supply house.
52. Vermiculite (expanded mica)	Building supplies.

* For smaller quantities write: Masco Chemical Co., 58 John Hay Ave., Kearny, New Jersey.

53. vinyl acetate	See "Vinylite."
54. vinyl chloride acetate	See "Vinylite."
55. Vinylite (Union Carbon and Chemical Corp.)	The Chemicals Division of the Union Carbide Corp. N.Y.C., N.Y. or a chemical supply house.
56. xylene	Chemical supply house.

B. Bibliography

Allyn, Gerould. *Basic Concepts of Acrylic Resin Emulsion Technology.* Philadelphia: Rohm & Haas Co., 1956.

Architectural Record. "Murals of Acrylic Plastic Introduce New Art Technique." *Architectural Record,* Vol. 124, No. 3, Sept. 1958.

Barzun, Jacques. "Modern Architecture: The Road to Abstraction." *Columbia University Forum,* Vol. IV, No. 4, Fall, 1961.

Brooks, Leonard. *Oil Painting . . . Traditional and New.* New York: Reinhold Publishing Corp., 1959.

Cary, Joyce. *The Horse's Mouth.* New York: The Universal Library, Grosset & Dunlap, Inc., 1957.

Cennini, Cennino. *The Craftsman's Handbook.* Trans. Daniel V. Thompson, Jr. New York: Dover Publications, Inc., 1933.

Cope, Dwight, and Floyd Dickey (ed.). *Cope's Plastics Book.* Chicago: The Goodheart-Willcox Co., Inc., 1957.

Davis, Gladys Rockmore. *Pastel Painting.* New York & London: The Studio Publications, Inc., 1943.

Doerner, Max. *The Materials of the Artist.* New York: Harcourt, Brace & World, Inc., 1934.

Duca, Alfred. *Polymer Tempera Handbook.* Somerville, Mass.: Polymer Tempera, Inc., 1956.

Grosser, Maurice. *The Painter's Eye.* New York: The New American Library, 1956.

Gutiérrez, José. *From Fresco to Plastics, New Materials for Easel and Mural Painting.* Ottawa: The National Gallery of Ottawa, Canada, 1956.

Mayer, Ralph. *The Artist's Handbook.* New York: The Viking Press, Inc. Revised Edition, 1957.

Shahn, Ben. *The Shape of Content.* New York: Vintage Books, 1960.

Vasari, Giorgio. *The Lives of the Painters, Sculptors, and Architects.* 4 vols., New York: E. P. Dutton & Co., Inc., 1927.

Index

A

Abstract Expressionists, 4, 6, 29, 37
Acetone, industrial, 108
Acrylic plastics, 43
Acrylic polymer tempera medium, 48, 49
Acrylic resin emulsions, 43
Acrylic resin painting, 42 (fig.)
Acrylic resin paints, 14, 41–43, 53, 80–90
    varnish for, 90
Acrylic resins, 23, 41, 48, 81
    characteristics of, 43
    development of, 41–43
"Action" painting, 5, 37
Adherence ability of polymer tempera, 59
Alla prima painting, 34
Allyn, Gerould, 41n., 43n.
"Anti-design," 6
Aqua-Tec, 48, 72, 80
Architectural Record, 73n.
Artificial light and traditional north light, 6
Artist's Handbook, 24n., 25n., 28n.
Artists Technical Research Institute, Inc., 61
A.Y.A.F. and A.Y.A.T. forms of vinyl acetate medium, 107–108

B

Baekeland, Leo H., 39
Bakelite, 39
Baltimore Museum of Art, 81
Barniz Sellador, 79
Barzun, Jacques, 12n., 123n.
Bas-relief surfaces, 53, 64
Basic Concepts of Acrylic Emulsion Paint Technology, 41n., 43n.
"Betrothal of the Arnolfini" (Van Eyck), 32
Binders:
    modern synthetic, 2
    in traditional media, 2
Bittleman, Arnold, 21
Bocour Artists Colors, Inc., 48, 80, 82, 90
Bocour, Leonard, 44, 80, 81, 82, 85, 89
Borden Company, 46
Botticelli, Sandro, tempera painting of, 16
Boucher, François, chalk drawings of, 20
Bouguereau, Adolphe William, 4
Braque, Georges, 4
Brooklyn Polytechnic Institute, murals at, 73
Brooks, Leonard, 92
Burri, Alberto, 37

129